Recruiting and Retaining a Diverse Workforce

New Rules for a New Generation

Natalie Holder-Winfield

FIRST BOOKS

PORTLAND • OREGON

FIRSTBOOKS.COM

www.firstbooks.com

ISBN-13 978-0-912301-80-8
ISBN-10 0-912301-80-5

Publisher: First Books

Printed in the U.S.A.
All paper is acid free and meets all ANSI standards for archival quality paper.

Table of Contents

ACKNOWLEDGMENTS

One of my mother's favorite sayings is "nothing ever happens before its time." I thank her so much for teaching me to live by this mantra. Subconsciously, it taught me the virtue of patience.

Writing a book requires more patience than I ever imagined. I was under the false impression that you sat down, wrote until you reached your desired page count, and then book publishers would come knocking at your door. Ok, I am exaggerating, but I thought that the process was less esoteric than it really is. From the conceptualization stage to actually writing out my ideas and then working through the publishing process, it all can feel like a waiting game. The words never come fast enough, you get tapped out of ideas, and figuring out publishers is like a maze.

I have to say, though, the process was worth it and I had the best people in my corner. To ensure that I don't forget to thank anyone, I want to thank all of my friends and family who encouraged me to continue my work with QUEST and to probe and be curious about people and how they worked. My husband, Gary Holder-Winfield, was more supportive than I could have asked for. From reading my manuscript countless times to keeping me motivated, he never complained.

Initially, this book was supposed to be a conference paper that would accompany my presentation at the Seventh Annual International Conference on Diversity in Communities, Organizations and Nations. The people I interviewed helped me to turn a 20-page paper into a 200-page book. You know that I would thank you by name, but I promised to protect your identities. You all carved out valuable time from your schedules to help me learn more about your experiences and hopefully provide the world with a different perspective about handling diversity and communication in the workplace. Thank you for meeting with me at coffee shops, talking to me at work while in the middle of closing a deal, and answering interview questions while you were traveling for business. Thank you for squeezing me in.

My peer editors were just as great. Thank you for helping me to focus on the important issues. Your feedback, which at times was hard to handle, really made my project more of a book than a research paper. Sheila Foster, Kathleen Brady, and those of you who volunteered to do double duty as an interviewee and a peer editor, thank you for investing your time and energy in me.

Speaking of feedback, I truly have to thank the team at First Books. From two-hour conversations with Linda to finalize the editing, to Jeremy working with me on a book title, to Masha putting together the layout in breakneck speed, all of you were first-class professionals during the process.

I dedicate this book to all of you who touched and inspired my work.

INTRODUCTION

Everything happens for a good reason.

In 2006, eight of my colleagues and I said hello to our new lives. We had all worked for law firms and decided to leave for various reasons. I worked for Outten & Golden, one of the best employment law firms representing employees in New York to pursue my interest in diversity training. Before I joined the firm, I had part-time projects as a trainer and I really enjoyed the work. I finally reached the point where I could not think of a good reason to delay pursuing my dream of creating diversity and career management training programs. However, my colleagues had more passionate reasons for wanting to start a new chapter in their professional lives.

On paper, these women had it all. They graduated from Harvard, Columbia, and other great law schools that most people could only dream of attending. They worked for the who's who of international New York law firms. They traveled extensively for business, bought beautiful brownstones in Brooklyn and Harlem, owned wine collections, and rounded out their lives by having adorable children. However, they could not wait to escape from their law firms.

We started a five-year group where we would be accountable to each other in reaching the plans we set for ourselves for the year 2011. At our first dinner meeting, I heard stories that could have filled the pages of Ron Shapiro's bestselling book *Bullies, Tyrants and Other Difficult People*. These women told me about working all night to complete a writing assignment, on their birthday, only to have their boss scream at them for how they stapled the document. They told stories about their co-workers actively leaving them out of the social network, and how partners would pick their favorites for assignments and outings—favorites who were rarely women, people of color, or a combination of the two. Rather than wait for the firm to tell them that they were not named a partner, they thought, "Life is too short. I am too talented. I'm going to live my life to the fullest by doing what I've always wanted to do." These epiphanies gave birth to a real estate practice, a criminal and immigration practice, and a divorce law practice.

I found their stories intriguing. Although I practiced law for seven years, I never worked in a large law firm. I always worked in smaller, more relatively nurturing environments. Their stories were enlightening not only for me but for each other. Many of us wished that we had known these stories before we even went to law school. Not that we would have decided against becoming lawyers; we just would have been better prepared. We would have realized that becoming a law firm partner requires more than just having good grades and doing great work.

Little did we know, we were walking statistics. That same summer, every woman of color I knew at a law firm was buzzing about "the study." The American Bar Association's Commission on Women in the Profession conducted groundbreaking research about the legal profession that could not go unnoticed. According to the study, almost 85% of women of color leave their law firms within eight years of being hired. This was such a startling statistic because most international law firms require associates to commit eight to ten years of their lives to the firm before they will be considered for partnership. The study exposed an obvious truth that most women of color already knew; most of us are not on partnership track. Whether we hopped from firm to firm, left law firms to become in-house counsel, or simply left the law altogether, we just didn't meet that eight-year of commitment with one law firm. Everyone wanted to know why.

Professionals across the board were curious because as they looked around their own professions, they also noticed a dearth of women of color and other minorities in leadership positions.

My friends in academia, the human services, investment banking, medicine, and a number of other fields thought that attorneys had it good and were eager to find out why most women of color left law firms. They thought about the six-figure salaries. They heard stories about lavish summer associate outings to Napa Valley, California, and other plush locales. Attorneys are often at the forefront of society. We handle entertainment, white-collar crime and most other headline news–making cases. Johnny Cochran's work—and showmanship—during the O.J. Simpson case told the world just how important a good attorney is to a client. The attorney life looked glamorous to everyone on the outside, but most women of color in law firms knew a different story.

Although the ABA report started to pull back the curtain on the atrocious experiences of women of color within law firms, it didn't have the impact I thought it would in white male circles. Many white men I spoke with, who had also left large law firms, were not moved or surprised by the statistics. Although the study revealed that 50% of women of color reported that they experienced demeaning comments and harassment compared with only 3% of white men, white men still felt that law firms are evil places where everyone is mistreated. In other words, the women of color were treated no differently than anyone else in a firm who was not tapped as a star by the leadership. The white men who privately shared their true feelings about the report brushed it off. They cited their experiences of being mistreated and not being offered partnership, and they were not women of color. To them, the ABA study didn't reveal any secrets about Oz.

To a certain extent, these men were right. Some managers are equal opportunity jerks. They do not respect their workforce and do not know how to motivate their people to achieve greatness.

However, here we had quantitative research showing that women of color are dramatically more susceptible to adversity in the workplace than their male counterparts. How do we get white men, who are decision makers and co-workers, to see that there is a problem? How do we get them to acknowledge that women of color and other minorities in the workplace are still denied equal access to opportunities?

Training the Competition's Talent

Fortunately, most businesses have acknowledged that there is a retention crisis within their diversity plans. I recently facilitated a retention strategies breakfast at a corporation headquartered in Connecticut where human resource and diversity coordinators from various Fortune 500 companies attended to learn more about each other's challenges and successes with managing retention of diverse talent. The breakfast covered some of the main reasons why employees leave, and a few companies were very vocal about how they have tried to stop hemorrhaging their talent.

Halfway through the breakfast, I noticed something troubling. The corporate officers were starting to feel comfort in knowing that no one company was immune to the retention issues. They were all struggling with the same problems. I could see them getting cozy with the idea that this was a problem without any solutions. However, companies do not grow when they accept defeat. As the consultant Ram Charan—who relies on Sanskrit teachings—tells his corporate clients, "fear, anger and laziness are the downfalls of human beings." Similar to any other business initiative—creating a new product, keeping costs down, finding new ways to converge technologies—this was a challenge that corporations should meet head on. This was a time to try to take the lead.

If these officers gave up and just accepted that they could not keep their talented employees from all different backgrounds, it would become a self-fulfilling prophecy. They would train their employees of color, women, and other minorities to become the best, but the best who would be looking for a new opportunity elsewhere. Basically, the company would be giving the competition its most valuable resource—its employees.

IS THIS JUST HAPPENING TO ME?

As I thought about writing this book, the number one goal was awareness. I wanted to go beyond my five-year group to see if people in other professions encountered similar adversity and how they handled it. I also wanted to create a similar supportive place for marginalized professionals that my five-year group had created for me. I wanted minority professionals to know that they were not alone.

I approach diversity training by using the employment

laws as a parameter for understanding one's rights and responsibilities in the workplace, but then I really work with people to devise creative strategies for handling workplace conflicts. While I'm far from knowing all of the answers, I was on a mission to get as many answers as I could.

While my goal was not to engage in an empirical study about the workplace—I'll leave that up to the researchers—I developed a theory. As I listened to my friends and colleagues, read magazine interviews about successful CEOs, and attended professional trade organization conferences, I heard common themes in experiences. While the circumstances may have been different in detail, they were similar in essence. When individuals encountered adversity, they found themselves as outsiders. Many diversity programs focus on inclusion and making people feel like true contributors to the company or organization. As they say, this is where the rubber meets the road in terms of workplace diversity and developing retention strategies; the more integral individuals feel in an organization the more likely they are to stay in that organization.

If you can detect a situation, often you can correct it. For instance, if you know and can articulate the elements of sexual harassment, most often you can develop strategies to correct it. So I started thinking about what makes a person feel like an outsider? What are the encounters that make us feel as though we are the intended guests at a dinner party instead of accidental interlopers?

For months, I interviewed the best and the brightest in various professions. I discriminately scanned by rolodex for people who were at the top of their professional career. I called and emailed the rising stars I had read about in magazines and newspaper articles and interviewed them. I had only one initial question: Have you ever felt like an outsider? With my handheld tape recorder, I taped over 50 hours of conversations and transcribed them all. Some interviews took 15 minutes while others were over an hour. Often those interviewees who required the most convincing to participate found the interview cathartic. I could hear how they were thinking aloud, sometimes for the first time, about an incident that really affected them. After many of the interviews, the interviewee would make me promise to provide them with the results of my findings. They wanted to know the same things I set out to learn. They wanted to know if they were the only person who had encountered a situation and if they were not, they wanted to know how their contemporaries handled adversity with style and grace.

There is good news and not-so-good news. The good news is that people have developed successful mechanisms for handling the situation of being an outsider. The common theme that ran through their stories is that there are basically ten situations that people in the minority encounter. Everyone should know about these situations to detect and correct them. I'm sure that you have already guessed the not-so-good news. The not-so-bright side of my project revealed that there is still unfairness and intentional harm in the workplace. Most of the people I interviewed told me that they had been treated unfairly because of their race, gender, sexual orientation, or other personal characteristic. I will not give up hope, though, that change is possible.

I'm not sure if there are any secrets or magic bullets to increasing the retention of women, people of color, gays, people with disabilities, and all other groups that have been historically underrepresented. Inevitably, as a diversity consultant, my clients ask me whether I have the answer to this million-dollar question. I wish that I did, because apart from being able to finance that island (yes, island) in the Caribbean that I have always wanted to buy, I would be improving the lives of countless professionals who deserve better in the work-place. As an employment attorney, it was always my goal to put myself out of business, and the same applies as a diversity consultant. My goal is to change enough workplace behaviors such that there really is equal opportunity and access in the workplace. This book is just one more step in the direction in reaching my goals.

Laying the Foundation

Why Can't We Keep Them?

Have you ever had an "aha" moment or a life-altering moment where inspiration, a sense of mission, and self-motivation unexpectedly greeted each other and conspired to bring you closer to fulfilling your life's purpose? My "aha" moment in 2005 carried my life in a more fulfilling direction than I could have ever imagined.

At the time, I was an employment attorney who occasionally created employment education programs through the consulting firm, QUEST Diversity Initiatives. These programs educated employees and students about their rights and responsibilities in the workplace and gave them strategies for resolving workplace conflicts.

A bar association in Louisiana learned about my work and asked me to create a diversity training program for law firms in New Orleans. Although the program would cover various aspects of diversity—sexual orientation, gender, age, and workstyles—the most pressing issue facing the bar was race relations between black and white attorneys. New Orleans, pre–Hurricane Katrina, was demographically a majority black city, but most of the major law firms did not have many, or any, African-American partners. Firms were able to recruit, but not retain, black lawyers. On average black lawyers spent three years with a firm and then moved on. Whether they went to competitor firms, the government, opened their own firms, moved out of the city, or left the law altogether, most decided against pursuing a partnership track with a major law firm.

Partnership track is like reaching the "Promised Land" in a law firm. As an equity partner, you are a member of the firm's management and leadership. You get to share in the firm's profits—which can reach the millions—dole out assignments and set the firm's policies. Some associates have likened working at a firm, and never being made a partner, to "slave labor." So why would anyone leave a firm before making partner? How could a city where blacks made up the majority of the population have such a disproportionately low number of African-American law firm partners? Peculiar, but not unusual.

Before I develop any training project, I like to get a feel for the employment landscape from the people most closely related to the situation. Because this was a city-wide training that would involve a variety of law firms, I spoke to a broad spectrum of local experts. I talked with solo practitioners as well as law firm partners, law school counselors, and African-American associates at large law firms.

A small random sampling of highly regarded attorneys of color in the city shared stories that sounded as though they came from the pre–Civil Rights era. While most law firms, nationwide, struggle with improving their diversity initiatives, the lawyers I spoke with worked for firms that did not even have a clear and concise diversity plan. The attorneys' stories ranged from obvious exclusion to blatant discrimination. One attorney even told me that a law firm partner called him the "N" word at the firm's holiday party. Most of the attorneys told me about instances of being ignored by partners and associates such that they perceived that there were limited opportunities to becoming a partner at these large law firms. I was shocked by all of these stories but I was really floored by how recently all of these events took place. All of these attorneys were born after 1970, and these occurrences took place between 1995 and 2005.

All the lawyers I talked with had bounced around from law firm to law firm until they found their fit—at least for the time being. Some of the attorneys admitted that they were at firms which were merely a momentary stop on their journey to career happiness. They landed at firms that were just as bad as the ones they had left but were willing to tough it out until they saved enough money or gained enough skill in a particular practice area. It was only a matter of time until they jumped to another firm. Some of the attorneys were so disgusted by their big law firm experiences that they started their own firms and had no regrets. One solo practitioner proved that he had the business savvy to became a rainmaker for a law firm. In fewer than five years he built a million dollar book of business. Ultimately, every attorney found a way to turn what could have been a lemon into lemonade by carving out his or her own career path.

Once I gathered enough information, I wove in the local attorneys' stories with actual employment discrimination cases to create video vignettes that realistically depicted the law firm environment for attorneys of color in New Orleans. Set in a fictional law firm, the vignettes followed Frances, a fictional woman attorney, as she navigated the firm as the lone summer associate of color. (Summer associates are law students who work in law firms during the summer to test out whether they want to work for that firm after they graduate.) The video explored how the law firm's hiring committee doubted Frances' abilities and required her to meet higher standards—which Caucasian associates bypassed—before the firm would extend a job offer to her; how she was not invited to the firm's traditionally male-only golf outing; and how she was even excluded from business meetings. Although I purposely gave Frances enough character flaws such that there was room to debate whether she contributed to her firm treating her like an outsider, it was clear that Frances did not enjoy working for the firm.

I had planned, as I normally do, to use the QUEST Diversity Initiatives method—getting participants to Question their Understood Established Societal Training—to engage the attendees in a problem-solving session to design a diversity plan that would improve Frances' law firm experience, but I had a problem I didn't anticipate.

As the training progressed I realized that many of the law firm partners, most of whom were white men in their 50s, and law firm professional development managers, most of whom were white women in their 50s, expressed that they had no idea that many of Frances' experiences existed.

Many acted as though Frances' encounters, which were primarily based on the true experiences of the city's African-American attorneys' survival stories, could not happen. Many of the law firm partners in attendance indicated that since their firms had formal mentoring programs, situations like those depicted in the video could never occur in their firms. For example, an African-American associate would never be excluded from a firm-sponsored golf outing because *all* associates were invited to attend the same events. However, the partners could not figure out why *all* of their black associates left the firm before they were eligible for partnership.

Suddenly, a genuinely frustrated partner asked the pivotal question that many organizations struggle with, "How do we keep them?" I could tell that he sincerely wanted to solve the attrition dilemma with associates of color, but even his question suggested the problem. Even though I knew what he meant to ask was, "How do we keep our talented attorneys?," his question reflected that attorneys of color were still viewed as "other" people in his firm. Associates of color were not a part of the "we" but were viewed as "them."

Why didn't the law firm partners and professional development managers seem to know about the stories of disrespect, harassment, and discrimination featured in the video? As I gathered background research for the program, I found it fascinating how open all of the attorneys were with me. I did not know any of the people I spoke with and we did not meet face to face until the day of the training. All of our conversations prior to the training were by telephone or email.

Yet, they shared very intimate thoughts and experiences with me as to what precipitated their decisions to leave their respective firms. Although they did not name names, it didn't take a forensic scientist to reconstruct their resumes and figure out who their former employers were. In a city as small as New Orleans, where everyone knows of everyone, the skeletons are not hard to find. It was obvious that there was no transparent information exchange between the attorneys of color and the law firms.

WHY I WROTE THIS BOOK: THE VALUE OF UNDERSTANDING CULTURAL DIVERSITY THROUGH GENERATIONS X AND Y'S PERSPECTIVE

During the program I noticed that there was not only a racial divide but also a generational divide between the associates of color and the leadership handling attorney development. Most of the attorneys of color were between 26 and 36 years old, while the partners and professional development managers were 50 years and older.

After the program, I wanted to read more about the overlay of generational differences and ethnic and gender diversity. As I perused bookstore shelves for books about diversity in the workplace, I noticed a common theme. There were very few books that covered the overlay of cultural and generational diversity. Most of the diversity books either covered generational differences or race, ethnic, and gender differences. Many studies have been conducted to quantify and define Generations X and Y's traits and characteristics. (Generally speaking, Generation X covers those born between 1964 and 1979, and Generation Y covers the period from 1980 through 1995.) Usually, research about generational differences is mutually exclusive from diversity research that focuses on women and ethnic minorities. Very few Generation X and Y studies address how younger employees, particularly employees of color such as Frances, are treated in the workplace and how they respond, especially to discrimination and harassment.

Plus, most of the books I found were written by people with over "twenty years of experience" in human resources or an employee relations field. However, none of these books were written by people who were close to twenty years old. Very few of these books and studies spoke to me. I was born in the late 1970s and I'm a proud member of Generation X and a cusp member of Generation Y. It seemed incomplete to discuss diversity in today's workplaces without gathering the thoughts, feelings, and suggested solutions of today's younger professionals.

Based on resources gathered by the Association of Career Professionals International, the profiles of the three main working generations reveal dramatically different events that shaped and defined them:

COMING OF AGE EVENTS

Baby Boomers
- The "Me" generation: self-centered, but optimistic and idealistic
- Nostalgic
- Fought in or organized opposition to Vietnam
- Beatlemania and modern clothes
- Believe the world can be changed
- "50 is the new 40"

Generation X
- Latchkey kids
- The space shuttle explosion
- The fall of the Berlin Wall and the end of the Cold War
- Inflation and recession economies
- Divorce rates grew as did significant alternatives to traditional marriage—from remaining single to same-sex couples to merely "living together"
- More global, technologically oriented, and culturally diverse than the generations before them

Generation Y
- Shaped by the terrorist attacks of September 11th and the shootings at Columbine and other American schools
- Exhibit an altruism that embraces the environment, poverty, and community problems
- Parents, family, religion, and generosity are central to this generation
- Celebrate diversity—display a high degree of acceptance towards different cultures, lifestyles, and behaviors

- Self-inventive/individualistic

WORK STYLES

Baby Boomers
- Internet savvy
- Attitude toward work: a career for 53%; just a job for 24%
- Independent
- Work long hours
- Struggle with work-life balance
- Overachieving
- Multi-taskers

Generation X
- Internet savvy
- Embrace risk and prefer free agency to loyal corporatism
- Sometimes criticized as "slackers" yet are widely credited with a new growth of entrepreneurship
- Jump from job to job, are unwilling to conform to organizational demands that do not suit them, and leave jobs that bore them and are not fun
- Adopted the philosophy there are "no guarantees," and they are not interested in working their way up
- Want to be valued immediately for their skills
- Require more coaching and feedback from their supervisors than previous generations

Generation Y
- Raised with the internet
- Work on their own terms—command of technology and having experienced affluence so early in life put them in a unique position to negotiate those demands

- Join organizations not because they have to but because they really want to and because something significant is happening there
- Pragmatic and hard-working
- Among those 18–24, about 45% are employed full-time and 22% are employed part-time

So, as diversity officers develop diversity and inclusion plans, why should they be concerned with how Generations X and Y react to adversity in the workplace? It is not as though Generations X and Y are the first generations to encounter adversity in their professional lives. The American worker has always faced challenges in the workplace. Cultural icons like Mr. Slate from "The Flintstones" and Larry Tate from "Bewitched" were menacing employers who told their employees, "you're fired," as often as they said, "hello." My generation is not the first to work for bosses with hostile attitudes toward their workers.

Aha! Many employers don't realize the extent to which Generations X and Y think about and react differently to discrimination than our parents do. Technology has exposed the racism, sexism, and other types of discrimination that our parents suspected in their workplaces and society. We grew up watching proof of discriminatory conduct. Television cameras, recording devices, and the internet gave us access to what happens behind the closed doors of the old boys' club. Once upon a time, the hard-working little guy was only able to speculate that he was continuously denied a promotion because of his race, ethnicity, or any other characteristic that the majority determined made him different and subsequently less qualified. Today, we have clear and crisp audio of Texaco executives disparagingly referring to African-American workers and describing their plot to keep them in their place. Today, we have footage captured by a cell phone of our favorite television actors calling African-American nightclub patrons the "N" word. When we watched the Rodney King beatings, our parents' stories of police brutality were confirmed. We watched news magazine programs like "20/20" conduct social experiments showing how a black male and white male tester, with the same educational and social pedigree, were treated differently. The black male tester did not receive the same jobs, favorable prices on vehicles, and access to New York City cab service as his white male counterpart. Minorities in Generations X and Y no longer merely talk of conspiracy theories about "the man." Thanks to the videos on YouTube and Google, today we often know who the man is and what he looks like.

How can organizations create meaningful diversity plans and programs for the next generation if they do not have a clear sense of how minorities in Generations X and Y interpret and react to discrimination in the workplace? As Generations X and Y are positioned to imminently inherit the workplace when the Baby Boomer generation glides into retirement, it behooves organizations to examine the entire diversity picture.

When I speak to human resources, diversity, recruiting, and professional development managers, most are perplexed that their efforts to recruit, retain, and advance a diverse workforce have not reached the level of anticipated success. Many of these managers work from defeated notions that diversity in the workplace is impossible because people will never change. Some create programs like sponsoring a "Soul Food" day in the company cafeteria to celebrate Black History Month, and don't understand why their employees of color are more often offended than impressed. Some feel that they have done their job by creating affinity groups, and believe that talented students and employees from underrepresented backgrounds will automatically consider them a company that embraces diversity. Other organizations have started to believe that they cannot keep their talented employees of different backgrounds because they are leaving for more money. Some organizations are even under the delusion that minorities do not want to work in high-paying competitive environments because they will be the only gay person, or Asian person, or any characteristic you can find to fill in the blank. And some organizations try to blame their shortcomings on the numbers and claim that there are not enough qualified candidates. Yet, none of these approaches to diversity recognizes or addresses the workplace adversities that are unique to people of color, women, and other traditionally underrepresented groups.

Aha! There was a need to inform companies and managers about diversity from not only a generational perspective but also a cultural perspective.

The maverick nature of today's employee should signal to organizations that today is a different day. When the typical career path of joining a firm and staying until offered partnership seemed impossible or improbable, those black attorneys from New Orleans I interviewed quickly reacted to the situation and created other opportunities. In contrast, Boomers and previous generations typically spent their entire lifetimes working for companies often because they were trapped by the golden handcuffs—the metaphor used to describe the miserable sacrifices our parents and grandparents made to stay with an employer because of a high salary. Yet, Generation X and Y attorneys of color found ways to survive and thrive. Consistent with the attorneys of color in New Orleans, I constantly meet young people who boldly jump from one organization to the next. Some even left Corporate America to start their own ventures before they reached the senior leadership level. How were they able to escape the golden handcuffs?

As Bruce Tulgan, an expert on Generation X and Y, wrote in *Winning the Talent Wars* (W.W. Norton & Company, 2001), "In the new economy, the best people are the most likely to leave. Why? Because they can. And they are likely to leave long before they've paid their dues or even paid a return on your recruiting and training investment."

This book creates an information exchange between perplexed professional development managers and the post–Baby Boomers. I wanted to give organizations that truly care about diversity—or should care because it affects their bottom line—the opportunity to see how and where they should change course. I wanted to strip organizations of the excuse that there are not enough talented women, people of color, gays and lesbians, and people of different underrepresented backgrounds to hire. There are enough of us! It's just that organizations do not know how—or are unwilling—to implement measures to keep us.

THE OUTSIDER MODEL: A NEW PARADIGM FOR EXAMINING INCLUSION

⇢⇤ ⇥⇠

"He who feels it, knows it."

Robert Nesta Marley, Reggae Artist

⇢⇤ ⇥⇠

Since most organizations recognize how important diversity is in the workplace, I will not spend much time laying the foundation for the business case for diversity. With initiatives like the Call to Diversity, a mission statement signed by over 100 corporate general counsels demanding that law firms become more diverse, most organizations are beyond the point where they need to be convinced of the importance of diversity. They understand the economic importance of making sure that they have the most talented workforce that reflects the diversity of America's marketplace. The challenge for most of the organizations I have met with is determining how to effectively allocate resources to a diversity initiative that will help meet their goals.

While diversity encompasses all types of differences in our qualities and attributes, most organizations focus on achieving racial, cultural, and gender equality and inclusion with their diversity programs. On the surface, we know that it is wrong to discriminate against people based on their immutable characteristics, but many individuals still harbor and act upon their prejudiced beliefs. We still live in a society where Don Imus, a multimillion-dollar–earning radio host, feels comfortable enough to call the women on a predominantly black basketball team "nappy-headed hos." Or where Neil French, a senior advertising executive for the biggest advertising agency in the world, was ousted for openly declaring at an industry conference that "Women don't make it to the top because they don't deserve to. They're crap!" While workplace discrimination and harassment are often much more subtle, there is still the challenge of overcoming prejudices and preferences. Most organizations understand that there are challenges in trying to get managers to treat all of their employees equally regardless of what they look like. They are trying to figure out how to get that 55-year-old white male manager to make the only Asian woman in the office feel like she is a valued part of the team.

Most diversity programs try to change behaviors through awareness and sensitivity training, and some organizations resort to scaring people into changing. Shaming and scaring usually do not change people; they only force people to become more creative in hiding their biased tendencies. Let's try a different approach to encourage people to take a closer step toward embracing diversity.

Aside from downright mean and intentional conduct from people who have no interest in increasing diversity, most people fail to create inclusive cultures for two reasons. One explanation is that they do not realize how to relate to women, people of color, gays, and other minority groups. The second explanation is that they do not know what marginalization looks like for their employees and colleagues who have been historically underrepresented in the organization.

Usually, it is easier for people to truly understand and respect each other when they share a common experience, a common experience that makes it possible for them to relate to each other. Alumni associations, fraternities, and even weight-loss programs are premised on a model where people bond because they all shared a similar experience. Whether it was sharing the experience of living in the same dormitory, or being hazed by an overzealous pledge master, or knowing what it is like to crave a chocolate donut at 3 a.m. when dieting, people are better equipped to help and work with each other when they have shared an experience.

What is the common denominator experience that most of us can relate to regardless of race, gender, ethnicity, disability, or any immutable characteristic? At some point most of us have felt like the outsider, as though we did not fit in with a group. Have you ever been in a situation where you were the only person with (or without) a particular characteristic? Have you felt like the "only one" while riding on a subway or bus, or while driving through a different part of town? Were you the only person dressed inappropriately at an event? Many of us have felt as though we were not a part of a group because of our race, gender, ethnicity, color, disability, socioeconomic status, style of dress, political affiliation, you name it.

When you found yourself in a situation where you noticed that you were the only person with a characteristic, guess what? You were a person in the minority. How did you feel? Uncomfortable? Self-conscious? Be honest. As a young black woman I know that I have felt like an outsider (and have been an outsider) on many occasions.

Usually we feel as though we don't belong when we are a person in the minority and that feeling is only multiplied when someone tells us as much. Once it is confirmed that we are not wanted by a group, we lose interest and stop investing our time, energy, and passions in the group and ultimately look for ways to leave.

Building upon this framework where we can tap into the shared feelings of being a person in the minority, let's go one step further. Wouldn't it be even more powerful to find common threads of behaviors and conduct that make us feel excluded when we're the person in the minority? When we can easily identify exclusion, and categorize it, we have the ability to find successful remedies.

The medical world offers a helpful paradigm for thinking about diversity. When scientists want to find the cure to a rare medical condition, they first observe the patient and take into consideration all of the condition's symptoms. Once the doctor determines the root cause of the condition she can make a diagnosis and administer a cure. More important, once the doctor makes a diagnosis, she names the condition. By naming the condition, the doctor who discovered the condition and the rest of the medical community can quickly administer a cure if they see the same symptoms appear in another patient. Similarly, in the workplace, when we know the root cause for why a person feels excluded, a manager or the excluded individual can take steps to cure the situation. However, unlike doctors, the diversity management world has missed the extra step of naming the barriers to exclusion. We know what ails our environments, but we do not have a quick reference list of the barriers that most frequently affect our workplaces. This is where I saw an opportunity to make a difference and create a toolbox for managers and employees who sought to detect and correct exclusion in the workplace.

Although there are a million different types of behaviors that make us feel excluded, essentially, I noticed that there are ten different barriers to inclusion. I analyzed the employment discrimination case law, interviewed various marginalized employees, and gathered the visceral thoughts and feelings from close friends about their encounters with exclusion. Over and over again, many of the same themes kept popping up. Whether I was talking to a person in financial services or a television anchor, I found the same ten barriers to inclusion appear: 1) absence of informal mentoring; 2) lack of quality work assignments and promotions; 3) perceived underperformance; 4) insensitivity; 5) inability to recover from mistakes; 6) aggressive communication; 7) dual identity; 8) assumptions, slights, and other annoyances; 9) being the first and not having an extensive network; and 10) isolation and being ignored.

Understanding that most organizations learn best by using formats and models like Six Sigma or any leadership model from General Electric, I developed *Recruiting and Retaining a Diverse Workforce: New Rules for a New Generation.* The *New Rules* model compiles and describes the ten common experiences, thoughts, feelings, stories and issues people encounter that can make us feel excluded when we are in the minority.

While a 55-year-old male senior executive may not exactly understand the experiences of the only Asian woman in the office, he can relate to some of her experiences by tapping into his own feelings of when he was a person in the minority. He can also inform his actions, communications, and conduct by drawing from the testimonials and information that are shared in this book.

Recruiting and Retaining a Diverse Workforce is based on conversations and interviews with professionals from a wide range of fields. I spoke with lawyers (naturally), advertising sales executives, media personalities and executives, authors and editors, scientists, marketers, financial executives, accountants and so on to gather their experiences of being a person in the minority. The only consistent criterion for my interviewees was that each person had to have graduated from college and be employed at the time of the interview. The testimonials come from graduates of Harvard, Georgetown, Columbia University, and a number of other highly regarded schools. I wanted to be sure that the testimonials were gathered from an ostensible crème de la crème.

The people who shared their experiences and feelings did more than provide case studies so I prefer to see them as more than just research subjects. They are people. Their testimonials bring to life the common syndromes of workplace adversity and how sometimes the feelings of exclusion damage a person's self-esteem and sense of self-worth; understandably, I am sensitive as to how the interviewees are characterized. I want to ensure that you, the reader, understand the emotions underlying their employment dilemmas and complicated career decisions. The testimonials are invaluable for their honesty. The people I interviewed shared raw feelings and thoughts that most people would never share publicly as a speaker on a diversity panel (at least while sober). The professionals I interviewed are tired of feeling undervalued in the workplace and are eager to see change. They want to forge healthier relationships with their majority colleagues and managers. Some of the people I interviewed found ways to survive in environments that are far from welcoming, and developed survival mechanisms that are worth sharing. Some interviewees carved alternative paths for success and are working for organizations that fulfill their personal and professional interests. Through their testimonials, you will get a sense of historically under-represented employees' frustrations with working in environments where they had to constantly fight to get recognition for their hard work. You will also get a sense of their supervisors, who, even with an organization-wide diversity initiative, just didn't get it.

Recruiting and Retaining a Diverse Workforce is also intended to get people in the majority to identify with the feeling of exclusion. Throughout this book, people in the majority may feel as though they could have been telling the story in the testimonial because they too have experienced mistreatment and unfairness at the hands of a manager. However, members of the majority should understand that the disenfranchisement discussed in each testimonial happens with greater frequency and greater harm to your employees and colleagues of color, women, and other groups who are in the minority in the office. Readers in the majority should not stop at the point where they recognize the stories of disrespect, though. Try to dig deep and think about how you felt in a similar situation. Own those feelings and reactions and use them to guide your policies and future conduct. This will put you on the road to becoming a diversity ally. The goal is to create a new basis for people in the majority to understand the experiences of people in the minority. We want our brothers and sisters in the majority to not only sympathize with our experience but also empathize.

It may seem at times that my book is for lawyers. However, this book is for anyone who has ever felt alone in a discriminatory situation and anyone who seeks to become an ally in the quest for diversity. I apologize in advance for focusing heavily on the legal profession, but I just followed the conventional wisdom of writing about what I know best. As a lawyer, it was easy to use the legal profession to create examples and learning opportunities. I used the legal profession, which struggles to become more inclusive and diverse, as a glaring example of the pitfalls and barriers to creating more diverse environments. (For instance, according to an American Bar Association study, over 80% of women of color leave their law firms within eight years of practice.)

And lastly, I gathered a few expert opinions to weigh in on the dialogue. I spoke with authors, business school professors, and socially conscious entertainers to provide invaluable insights. At the end of Chapter 10, I provided space to allow you to collect your own thoughts on how you related to the issues featured in the chapter. Through writing, you may recognize your own feelings and start to develop solutions.

WHO SHOULD READ THIS BOOK?

For Diversity Managers

Initially, my target audiences were the professional development managers, diversity directors, and equal employment compliance officers for major corporations. While many seem committed to advancing diversity in the workplace, their programs and initiatives often miss the mark or lose steam.

⟶ ⟵

Consider 29-year-old Dale Johnson,[*1] a senior accountant for an international bank, who wants to see his firm succeed in its diversity mission but seriously doubts that his firm really cares about diversity. "When we talk about diversity at my company, it is all for show. Back in 2000, there was big talk about diversity, but I didn't see it. Diversity was more in theory than in practice. The retention rate of keeping people of color is not there. There was no desire to keep us. My company has a big diversity event and then you don't hear about diversity anymore. The people in the diversity positions change and then you have to reeducate the new person to the position. There was no succession planning for diversity officers. There was no one to push the diversity initiative. Diversity is like a wave. Things start to get better and then management loses its momentum. You want to know the funny thing? I got an email from a friend who informed me that my company is in the top 50 for diversity according to Diversity Inc. 2006. I always find it ironic. If we are in the top 50, it is only because of our retail business. Within the nonexempt positions and hiring ranks, diversity is lost. Diversity is a hot ticket item in the public, but once it dies down the company doesn't care anymore."

⇒ ⇐

Thousands of professionals who have been historically underrepresented in the workplace continue to leave companies, and Corporate America altogether, in droves because of lackluster efforts to create inclusive cultures. Employees can sniff out frauds and are able to detect when a company is genuinely committed to advancing equal opportunities for all of its employees. The testimonials from professionals who could easily be your employees (and in some cases were your employees) provide real and honest experiences that might give you a better sense of why your organization is not able to maintain a diverse working environment.

This book does not attempt to reinvent the wheel on sensi-

---

[1] An asterisk (*) denotes where an interviewee's name was changed to protect his or her identity.

tivity training. There are tons of exercises and training programs that teach students and employees how to treat one another in the workplace: workplace "dos" and "don'ts" programs. This book should be used to understand the stories behind the attrition numbers. It is a closer look at the employee who is sitting in an exit interview giving politically correct—and safe—answers. The stories should be used to understand how behaviors can affect others in spite of employing the "best" diversity efforts. The cross-section of professionals who shared their thoughts and ideas about the best and worst work environments provide insights for strengthening your own professional development and diversity programs.

For Mid-level and Junior Employees

Employees can learn a great deal from the interviewees' testimonials. For starters, you will realize that you were not the only person to experience isolation, a boss's aggressive conduct, and some of the other ten issues that minorities encounter. Many of the interviewees did not stay mad when things did not go their way in the workplace; they got smart. They devised strategies to take control of adversity and found profitable escape routes. The stories shared by the interviewees should be used by employee-readers to similarly take charge of their careers.

When I received feedback from my peer editors, the most notable reaction was surprise that organizations are really trying to attract and retain talented employees of all backgrounds. As a person who sits in planning sessions with various companies, I can tell you that there are organizations that are serious about increasing diversity. Some companies are spending enormous amounts of money to attract and retain traditionally underrepresented employees. It's just that sometimes organizations are misguided in their approach. The testimonials in this book share strategies that employees have used to successfully direct their company's efforts, strategies that you can use to influence and achieve change in your organization.

Recruiting and Retaining a Diverse Workforce is also intended to give professionals in the minority a basis for understanding that their experiences are sometimes shared by our straight white male colleagues. Sometimes the exclusion and lack of respect we feel in the workplace is not a result of our race, gender, ethnicity, or any other similar characteristic; it is sometimes a matter of poor management. The testimonials from our majority colleagues open up the dialogue about the workplace and have the potential to create powerful alliances in pursuit of change.

For the Students: Some Don't Know What They Don't Know

Many of the issues raised in the testimonials are also important for students because the interviewees tackled some of the age-old issues that students may one day encounter. Now is the time to prepare for your future.

Most colleges and universities focus on job placement, provide industry seminars and business seminars such as Dress for Success, but rarely do they provide programming that prepares their students for the realities of the workplace. Sure, students attend diversity panels and cocktail parties that inspire students and gloss over their ugly experiences. However, how often does the career services office host frank discussions about the disappointments, challenges, and adversity encountered by professionals in the minority?

As Malcolm Gladwell wrote in *Blink: The Power of Thinking without Thinking* (Time Warner Book Group, 2005), when people have a chance to understand and anticipate what is happening, their reactions are better informed. For instance, Gladwell describes a training exercise where bodyguards were put through a program referred to as "stress inoculation" (p. 238). The bodyguards were repeatedly put through a test where they were shot with plastic bullets and attacked by ferocious dogs. The test was conducted over and over again. The first time the bodyguards were faced with an emergency, they could not think straight and panicked. This panicked state was called "mind-blindness." However, by the second and third time the exercise was conducted, the bodyguards' reactions improved. The repetitive nature of the exercise combined with real-world exigencies took the surprise out of the encounters and the bodyguards were able to respond much better. The preparation gave the bodyguards the skill to "slow down, to keep gathering information." As Gladwell wrote, "This is the gift of training and expertise—the ability to extract an enormous amount of meaningful information from the thinnest slice of experience" (p. 241).

With advanced warning of the issues that members of the LGBT community, people of color, women, people with disabilities, and people from any other underrepresented backgrounds in the workplace encounter, today's students won't be as shocked and mind-blind if and when they encounter a similar situation.

This is not an easy topic to discuss without creating a structure around it so that it becomes educational and honest. It's also difficult to have these discussions without anonymity. Regardless of whatever mistreatment a person has endured, professionals know better than to name names under any circumstances. We do not tattle tell on those who made our lives miserable in Corporate America—and sometimes literally created our demise. We know that being a tattle-tale is career suicide.

⊶⊷

For instance, a black male law student asked Carmen Smith,* one of my interviewees, for her opinion about her former firm. Carmen loathed her former employer. For years, she witnessed the firm's partners speak abusively to African-American women and assign them to menial tasks. The firm eventually ousted her after a confrontation with an overbearing partner. (He yelled at her when she did not immediately return his telephone call on a Sunday evening.)

She asked me whether she should give the prospective candidate the typical song and dance about the firm, or should she tell him about her experience. I turned the question back to Carmen because deep down she knew what she had to do. (Plus, I told her that she had to watch what she said about her former firm since there was a non-disparagement clause in her severance agreement.) While she had a duty to warn this brother about the firm, she knew that she could not lambaste the firm even though she moved on; she has her own firm now and does not rely on her former firm for referrals or any type of support. Releasing her hatred about the firm would not have done her any good. It would have made her look petty and given how small this world can be at times, her words may have come back to haunt her. Instead, she gave the candidate polite answers with deeper meanings and facial expressions that communicated what she could not say. Carmen told the candidate, "XYZ firm met my financial needs but I found that after a while it did not meet my personal goals." If the candidate was listening closely he would have translated her response into, "The only reason I stayed with the firm was for the paycheck. Run away as fast as you can!"

⇥ ⇤

This book makes the next generation of employees aware of the discrimination and harassment that still exist in the workplace. As one of the experts I interviewed told me, professionals in the younger generations are "shocked" when they encounter disparate treatment at work. It is almost like a slap in the face. When I worked for the Commission on Human Rights, I felt most sorry for the clients who were highly educated and pursued high-level careers. They were the most mentally beaten down and physically drained when they finally stopped denying that they could be victims of discrimination.

⚬⚬⚬ ⚬⚬⚬

For Cynthia Turner, M.D.,* her galling experiences in the medical field are summed up perfectly by the title of Marvin Gaye's hit song, "Inner City Blues (Make Me Wanna Holla)." Dr. Turner's academic degrees from Cornell, Columbia, and Johns Hopkins did not give her the tools for handling subtle discrimination in academia or in the workplace. Not only is Dr. Turner one of a few black women in a male-dominated area of medicine but her youthful appearance only adds to her patients' and co-workers' misperceptions about her competence and overall worth as a doctor. Often second-guessed by her colleagues, she struggles for recognition. While most people would envy Dr. Turner's achievements, she sheds light on the ugly side of discrimination in the medical profession.

"My entire educational career I have felt like an outsider. Most of the pre-meds were predominantly Caucasian and Asian. There were times when I was not able to find partners to do lab projects. The exclusion got more intense in medical school because at that point people effortlessly form cliques and groups that form largely along racial lines. It just so happens that I would be the only black person on a rotation and everyone else would get together and study and prepare for the end of rotation exams or the clerkship exams. I would not be invited to participate in any of those study scenarios. I would not be invited to review sessions. I would not be privy to old exams or any sort of information that had been made available to facilitate studying.

"The residency level—it's indentured servitude—is essentially your first job as a doctor. For my residency, I actually trained at a NYC hospital that was a Jewish institution. It was a self-proclaimed Jewish institution in Manhattan, and informal hanging out among the staff or students, where I was not invited, was the kind of thing that I experienced.

"The feelings of exclusion were intense for me. I would walk into a room and sometimes people would speak Yiddish in my presence. Really, I can't participate in a conversation that's taking place in Yiddish. To say that it made me feel marginalized is a grotesque understatement. It made me feel less than human. It is one thing to know that you don't really matter to people, but it's another thing for them to illustrate it so dramatically. You don't even matter; you don't even count. It's offensive to any person, but it offends you on so many different levels. I have a Caribbean background and my parents are very proud Caribbean people. One of the most important things they instilled in me was pride. So it offends you even more given that pride was something that was drilled into you at a young age. It cuts you into the lowest common denominator. It puts you into an awkward position because how do you deal with and interact with people?

"A lot of people who interact with or deal with people of color think that we have a chip on our shoulder or that we have attitudes and that we essentially anticipate negative reactions. It becomes a self-fulfilling prophecy in a way. How do you subsequently interact with a person who made it clear to you that you don't matter, that you don't count, you are not a part of this unit? There were so many instances where I had to eat kosher food. I didn't have the guts to object because I knew how that would be viewed. It was clear that I was the visitor, so how would I, the visitor, be so brazen as to say I don't want to eat your kosher food? They just allowed me to be a voyeur but I was not allowed to participate in any real level. Obviously at that point, you cannot interact with people unless you have the ability to put aside those feelings of rejection. You can no longer interact with these people on a real basis.

"If I knew what I know now about practicing medicine I would not have become an anesthesiologist. It's not worth it. I come home in tears half the time because I don't know why people treat me this way. I'm just trying to go to work to do my job. I work my butt off. There are plenty of people who are just trying to get by. I have integrity and I work hard. I do my best. The hard time that I get in the process is hard to believe."

⟶⟹ ⟻⟸

For Dr. Turner and many other professionals in the minority, it was debilitating to realize that despite going to all of the right schools and working hard, she would still encounter discrimination and harassment. She and many other minority professionals were mind-blind. I can't tell you how many professionals I met who were so disgusted by their work experiences that they left their high-paying professions on Wall Street and became teachers or administrators in educational institutions. They thought that their Ivy League educations and hard work ethic would overcome discrimination. Many were actually in denial until it was too late.

Dr. Turner and the other professionals who shared their experiences throughout this book provide insights into the professions we idealize. The testimonials serve to refocus our attention on the realities that minorities still encounter. Students should not be swayed from pursuing medicine or any other career, but instead should be equipped to handle the situations raised in this book. The goal is to make the next generation of professionals less mind-blind than the previous generation.

CHAPTER I

ABSENCE OF INFORMAL MENTORING

⟶━◉ ◉━⟵

"A leader who does not produce leaders is not a great leader."

Ram Charan

⟶━◉ ◉━⟵

Do you remember your first day of work? Although you may have known how to research the latest news or create spreadsheets of yearly projections, you were practically useless until someone gave you your password and taught you how to access the company's computer network. You were also stuck until someone showed you where to sit, where to find office supplies, or how to complete your time sheet.

In addition to having someone help you master the technical administrative chores, you needed someone to introduce you to the organization's corporate culture. You needed someone to tell you about the boss's finicky likes and dislikes. You needed someone to help you understand when was the right time to propose a new idea and how to package it such that the department welcomed it with open arms. We all need someone to invest themselves in our success.

⇢⇒ ⇐⇠

Kara Brown,* a no-nonsense attorney for the federal government, is not blind to the investments an employer will make in an employee's success. Only in her early 30s, she has felt the difference between a boss who obsesses over her career versus a boss who couldn't care less. "I believe that as a professional whether it's law, business or medicine that you need a mentor. And it does need to be a formal mentor/mentee relationship but I think that you have to have someone who is senior to you. They need not be of your age, gender or race. But there needs to be someone in your professional career who is interested in your success, or else you are not going to be successful.

"I think that there are three kinds of people: people who are interested in your success, there are people who are indifferent, and there are some who are out to sabotage. Luckily, I have only met with the first two. I think that for my first two or three years with the government I worked for someone who was not only interested, but obsessed with my success such that I got great work. And when I did well on it, I got praise for it and my supervisors and colleagues knew about it. I came to have a reputation as doing good work, judges knew me, and colleagues knew me to be someone with a good head on her shoulders.

"In my last year and a half to two years working for this federal agency, I worked for someone who was more or less indifferent. He certainly did not mean me any harm but it was just a different dynamic. It was by no means intentional and I'm sure that he was happy to see me advance because actually under his tenure I received a promotion. But I do think it was a different relationship than with my previous supervisor.

"I've talked to my friends in the private sector and in the

government and it is absolutely true; you have to make sure that there is somebody who will give you good work and when you do well on it, let other people know that you did well. Otherwise, you can fall into the background and get lost in the cracks. I think that's true whether you're a minority professional or not. But, I think there's another level to it when you're a minority because when I sit across a desk from someone who's not black or a woman, there's an assumption that we don't have an understanding of one another because he or she doesn't look like me. And then we may talk, and find out that we have much in common and that we can work together and even hang out and have a great time. But from the moment I sit down, I don't look anything like you; you probably perceive my experience to be very unlike yours. I just think that you really need a cheerleader in your profession. It's too hard, it's too competitive not to.

"I've been abundantly blessed to have worked with people who were interested in my success or cheered me on. And even those colleagues or supervisors who were indifferent on the issue were always happy for me when good things happened."

❧ ❧

Very few organizations would argue the importance of mentoring for its ability to facilitate vital information exchange between senior and junior level employees. (Although they do disagree as to whether involuntary mentor-mentee pairings truly work.) Numerous articles have been written about formal mentoring programs and the radical results they have produced in the business world. Within the last 10 years, companies like AT&T's Consumer Sales Division, Boeing, and Deloitte & Touche have even created corporate universities that create structure for and give substance to the mentor-mentee relationship. These companies are willing to invest approximately $1,300 per employee to send their employees to corporate universities. According to a *Fortune* magazine article, corporations experience half the turnover rate and a 55% increase in performance by sending their managers to corporate universities.

However, are all employees given access to the same opportunities for mentoring? I have to say no. Regardless of formal mentoring programs, people still gravitate toward people they naturally like and create bonds with them, as expressed by Gladys Gossett Hankins, Ph.D., in her book *Diversity Blues: How to Shake 'em* (Telvic Press, Inc., 2000). The workplace is a lot like gym class in elementary school when you had to choose teams. Remember when your first pick was the star pitcher or point guard, then you chose your friends and the cool kids, and then you were *stuck* with who was left?

Many of us have not lost that innate desire to work with people we like for personal reasons. We choose to go to lunch with certain individuals as opposed to others because we may share common experiences with them and find it easy to talk politics, our love lives, or whatever with them. We invite co-workers to our summer barbecues because we may have gone to the same schools and share an alma mater. We invite the woman down the hall to the theater because we click. We invite the new guy to the Knicks game because we enjoy the same sports. Ultimately, we play and work with people we like.

⊷ ⊷

Benita Serles,* despite her cheery smile and good sense of humor, has always felt like the odd person out in her office because of her race. Although she feels as though she was welcoming to her colleagues—who were all white—she believes that they rejected her over and over again because they could not identify with her. "I've never worked in a situation where I was not in the minority. Being black is a constant. I always feel treated differently because I'm black. Sometimes it's very negative in an exclusionary way, other times it's just a sense of hesitation or not being included in any social events. I know that it's not exactly related to work but in the ultimate analysis it is. It's just not ever being invited out to the Thursday or Friday evening after-work party. There were times when someone made a mistake and asked, 'Are you going to the bar after work?' I felt out of the loop.

"It's not so much that I wanted to hang out with these people because I clearly did not, but the after-work gatherings are where relationships are forged. There is a lot of information that one can gather from these events. I never confronted the organizers of the events. I started to withdraw from the workplace and work on my way to get out. After a very long time, I got out. What happens when you leave one place for another with substantially the same diversity profile? I figured just a change of faces and maybe a slight change until one can't take it anymore and moves on yet again."

⊶ ⊷

As Benita noted, during these informal meetings—those "spur of the moment" outings—informal mentoring is taking place. When someone is tapped for an unspoken membership in someone's "in" club, he or she automatically becomes privy to vital information that is exchanged within that circle. The more elite the circle is, the more powerful the information exchanged will be. New projects and opportunities are discussed and assigned. What happens when some people are invited to impromptu lunches with supervisors and others are not? What happens when some people are continuously not invited to have drinks after work? Can a formal mentoring program overcome the advantages of informal networking?

⊶ ⊷

You could almost hear 32-year-old Shawna James* pound her fist on the conference room table as she exclaims, no. Shawna dabbled as an attorney for a large law firm before striking out on her own and starting a lucrative law firm practice. Her petite stature and Shirley Temple–style locks often fool her adversaries into thinking that she is a helpless and easy opponent. However, she is one of the Washington D.C. area's top-notch corporate transaction attorneys known for taking, and not giving away, the farm in a negotiation. Although it has been over five years since Shawna worked as an associate for a law firm, her matter-of-fact description of her summer associate experience and the lack of mentoring are crystal-clear memories that she will not soon forget. "I can recall not being mentored when I was working for a firm in the Midwest. I was going to school in Atlanta and I was an outsider because most of the people at the firm were from the area. I also noticed that there was a tight-knit connection between some of the attorneys and the summer associates who were not racial minorities.

"The racial minorities really didn't have anyone that they could call on. There was one African-American partner and one African-American associate out of over 150 attorneys.

"Obviously there were general opportunities that were given to all of the summer associates. We were all invited to the college world series, we were all invited to basic firm-wide events, but in terms of making personal connections or connections that would allow the attorneys and the partners an opportunity to get to know us on a personal basis—opportunities that would have given them additional information about making hiring decisions after we completed our summer associate positions—that did not happen. There were other non-black women summer associates who were offered those opportunities.

"There were a number of instances where there was a good ole boy network where some of the summer associates were getting invited to different events and opportunities and the minority attorneys were not. The minority summer associates were not provided the same opportunities. There were only two minority summer associates, so it was pretty clear when both of us were not invited to different events that attorneys had at their homes or different activities. That summer there were three (non–administrative staff) African-American women in the entire firm, myself included. I think that because of race some of the associates and partners did not feel comfortable with us or did not feel a connection to us, as they did with the other associates. It did not seem to me that they reached out to us in the same way. To a large degree the experience was expected. I anticipated being an outsider because I was not from the area and I didn't go to a college in the area. But there was another black female summer associate who was from the area who had a similar experience and had to push to make herself present and almost invite herself and demonstrate that she was available to get involved in the social activities, as opposed to just someone coming down the hall and saying, 'Are you available? We're going out to drink or we're barbecuing at someone's house. Would you like to come?' She really pushed forward and had to make people feel more comfortable with her being around. I think I took the opposite approach. I just disconnected from the situation and did my work but didn't really worry about the social aspect as much."

⊶ ⊷

Brock Douglas,* an African-American executive for an entertainment company, encountered a similar situation of exclusion when he worked in the automotive industry. To his surprise, and dismay, not even his M.B.A. from the Wharton School of Business kept him from being excluded from his supervisor's inner circle. "What's interesting is that things have gotten more subtle. Here's an example from a previous employer where there was this whole notion of not being in the circle. In a sense the circle was created by my boss where she handpicked people. When I joined her group, I came along as someone she had not handpicked. The organization was restructured and she had to deal with me. She had to accept me into the fold.

"Some of the resistance was that the people in her organization were white males and white females she was comfortable with. They would spend time together on the weekends, they would go out to dinner together and it felt like they were sons and daughters of the female boss who ran the group. In a sense, I felt like there were two things going on: (1) here I am an outsider because I was not hired by the boss and she had to attempt to accept me and (2) that aside, I still had the barrier of race. Probably even stronger, as a black man, there is an intimidation factor. I became a novelty in that situation and there was a challenge breaking through in that we did not have race in common.

"A particular example regarding resistance was travel. What expense-related events I traveled to and whether I needed to go to certain events was questioned. I felt like there was a level of scrutiny that was applied to me that was not applied to her close-knit group. I had to attend big entertainment and marketing events, like the Super Bowl, yet I was scrutinized. It wasn't like I was trying to attend the Essence Music Festival or BET or a niche ethnic marketing event. But, because my boss controlled the purse strings, she ended up making decisions about who, what, and where I attended events. I didn't see this type of questioning of my colleagues who weren't even going to events that were as germane to the business. It just felt like they had been going to these events for years and there was a wink and nod of approval. They were even going to events with her or they were going with people that she knew who were also in the circle, so it made it easier for her to say their events were legitimate but mine were not. I felt that it was unfair. I felt that it was a double standard. I felt that it was a zero sum game. It just felt like if I enjoyed myself or if it felt like the event I attended was going to be exciting or interesting, and she was not there or someone from her team was not there to oversee it, there was a question whether or not I should get a chance to do certain things. It felt like I needed to be chaperoned in a way that was not reasonable."

⟶⟦ ⟦⟵

How does one overcome an office clique that is created by upper management? It's bad enough when co-workers band together to exclude a minority employee, but it is even worse when it is the supervisor or owner of the company who decides to carve out social opportunities for some employees and not others.

⟶⟦ ⟦⟵

Lisa Charles* realized in her first real job after graduating from Duke University and Columbia University that the workplace was not created equally, especially if the boss cannot identify with you. Lisa worked for an international law firm and had every intention of becoming a law firm partner. While she kept her head in the books, she didn't realize, though, that law firm partners were tapping her colleagues on the shoulders for higher caliber opportunities.

Slowly, Lisa noticed that all work and no play was something that the partners determined as her destiny. By giving a little nudge to serendipity, Lisa was able to find another job where she now works for an organization that includes her in all types of workplace and social functions. When Lisa looks back at her experiences at the firm, she recognizes how a mentor would have brought her on a partnership track. "I should preface this conversation by saying that most of what I'll talk about is my experience at my former firm—an international law firm with over 500 attorneys—and not in my current job, because here I have not really felt like an outsider at all. There are a lot of minorities in my current job. It's mostly women and so there is a sensitivity here that was not at the firm.

"When I was at my firm I definitely felt excluded. It even goes back to when I was a summer associate. I was the only woman of color in a class of 35–40 summer associates. (There was an Asian guy. There was a black male and a Latina woman but they were first years in a special program for minorities.) That was very challenging and it was not as though I was overtly excluded, but there were very different social activities that I was not used to. Most of the social activities revolved around drinking. That was how folks socialized and got to know each other. I think you find that mostly among white men. There weren't social activities that I was more comfortable with.

Partners definitely made relationships with white male summer associates. Their relationships were based on so many things that were not about work. It was based on going out drinking together during lunch. It was based on going to each other's homes. Partners were inviting white male associates to their homes and I didn't even know about it until well afterward. People were taking associates out to lunch, informally. I was not a part of any of that. As summer associates, we would go out together and then occasionally the senior associates would take groups out so that they would get their lunches paid for.

"These relationships that were made between the partners and the associates were at the partner's initiative. It wasn't the summer associate going to the partner, which you sometimes hear you have to do. It was the partner inviting certain people. It happened among the white male members of my class, and it was about people feeling some sort of connection in terms of 'This person reminds me of myself when I was a first year' or 'This person reminds me of how I was when I was younger.' A white male is never going to say to a black woman, 'Oh, you remind me of how I was when I was younger.' There was no one in that leadership role that could say that about any person of color. That's part of the identity, right? And the familiarity? Race is part of that. Ethnicity is part of that. Being male or female is part of that. That's part of the identification. Unfortunately, there were no black women partners or black partners, period. There was one Asian partner who came later. Those informal mentorships started within the first six months of being at the firm. I was not a part of that.

"I didn't really know these informal relationships were going on until well into my second year. I didn't really notice it and I didn't realize how important it was. That's one of the things that if I could go back and do it again I would do differently—the politics of working at a firm. I didn't really appreciate how important the politics were. I didn't realize it was going on around me until it was too late. By the time I realized that people were forming these friendships and relationships that are much more beyond the business context, it was too late. It wasn't until I saw that there were one or two people who were identified in my class as 'really great people to work with' who I knew were not necessarily the smartest people. I worked with them, and I knew that their work was ok. They made mistakes when I was working with them. I began to see how certain people were given work because the people who were being promoted had the right people behind them. The people who are still at my former firm were people who were identified in their first year as people who were going to make it."

⚬⚬ ⚬⚬

Interestingly, when I suggest to companies that I include

mentoring advice in the employment education programs I have been hired to present, they confidently assure me that, "All of our employees have access to the same opportunities." These organizations believe that since they have mentoring programs, all of their employees have a mentor in the organization.

➝➡ ◉◄

Yet, as Kathleen McDonald* reveals, mentoring is sometimes based on what you look like and not necessarily who you are. Kathleen is a caramel-colored Caribbean woman who wears her hair naturally curly. Motivated to become an attorney because of the intellectual challenge it presented, she started her career path at Harvard Law School. She spent the earlier years of her career working for an international law firm in New York City where her office was ensconced in the center of Wall Street's wealth and bordered by the Statue of Liberty and the East River.

Although Kathleen's firm had a formal mentoring program, she noticed how many of the white partners informally socialized with her white male and female colleagues. "Whenever it came to social events, going to the theater, a sporting event like a golf event or so on, there was always a set group of individuals who were always sent invitations. But someone like myself was never on the invite because they just felt like the events were something I would not be interested in even though no one ever consulted me on the issue. I would hear about it after the fact, like, 'So and so went golfing with this particular partner.' The in crowd was white and willing. They were Caucasian for the most part and they said yes to everything. It didn't matter what it was, they were very good at schmoozing."

➝➡ ◉◄

Even though Kathleen was applauded for her work, she

was left out of those impromptu outings after work or on the weekends. These impromptu meetings were where her colleagues were creating closer relationships with the firm's leadership and were positioning themselves to work on the high-exposure projects. Kathleen's interactions with the partners were mostly limited to office meetings and a quick hello while passing in the hallways. After five years of working for this firm and feeling as though none of the partners had even an inkling of interest in her career, she left the firm to open her own law firm.

ADVICE FOR MANAGERS

Everyone I interviewed about mentoring expressed the importance of having a champion in the workplace. Incidentally, all of the people I interviewed worked for companies that had formal mentoring programs, yet there were noticeable differences in the way they were mentored versus their colleagues who resembled senior management.

Now, we are left with the question, how does an organization overcome the disparities caused by informal mentoring? How does an organization control natural bonds between senior and junior level employees and ensure that all employees are similarly mentored? As the senior level person, are you guilty of mentoring only people who look like you or your children? Do you only want to work with people who remind you of yourself?

As the testimonials indicate, subtle gestures to mentor some people and not others are blatantly obvious. When people feel overlooked or not invested in, they stop investing in the organization. Each time an employee leaves, it potentially costs the organization thousands in training and recruiting. Can your organization afford to lose valuable talent because a manager could not figure out how to schedule at least one out-ing—whether it's dinner or a casual office meeting—a month with all of the employees in a group or division with whom he or she closely works?

Informal mentoring is simple enough that any busy execu-tive can effectively master it. The gathering does not have to be anything extravagant. It could be as simple as a 15-minute one-Monday-a-month meeting in your office to discuss recent goings-on and make sure that your employees do not have any questions about work. Sometimes, but not all of the time, a telephone call will do. Or, it could be a matter of inviting the employee to your home to have dinner with your family. Of course, the more genuine and frequent the gatherings, the bet-ter, but employees will appreciate any effort toward mentoring that does not appear to be forced.

If you are a manager who has a reputation for inviting employees to events outside of the workplace, you should try to include a different mix of employees. As a manager, if you are concerned that you will not have anything to talk to your employee about, try talking about yourself. Junior and mid-level employees read books about captains of industry and are eager to learn how to advance within an organization. Surely, your employees would be interested to learn how you navi-gated your way through the organization.

ADVICE FOR PROFESSIONALS AND STUDENTS

When you notice that you are not invited to join an infor-mal mentoring relationship, the last thing you should do is throw a pity party for yourself. If you find yourself in Benita Serles' or Dr. Turner's situation where your colleagues are not inviting you to after-work social events or meetings, you should not be afraid to invite yourself. It is ok to ask your colleagues and manager, "Do you have room for one more?" Try to let people know that you are interested in going out with them. By taking the lead and suggesting a place where the entire group can socialize, you will naturally show your colleagues that you are approachable. Sometimes when we *think* that we do not want to be best friends with our managers and workplace colleagues, we subconsciously *act* like it.

Your career development is a two-way street and it is your responsibility to be proactive about getting what you want. It is a good idea to be courageous and let people know that you want their help. Sometimes you have to lead someone's hand in your direction in order to get them to help you. When you go to them for help and ask for their advice, people generally feel honored and will share valuable information with you. If you appear sincere and humble in your approach, more people may reach out to you.

As the employee, how do you get brought into the loop? An August 16, 2005, *New York Times* article, "Have You Heard? Gossip Turns Out to Serve a Purpose," underscored the importance of gathering crucial information about the workplace by using office banter to your advantage. The article confirms that "When two or more people huddle to share inside information about another person who is absent, they are often spreading important news, and enacting a mutually protective ritual that may have evolved from early grooming behaviors." Stay in the loop and speak to colleagues to find out who within the organization is good at mentoring and teaching. But remember to keep a safe distance from too much office gossip. In May 2007, four New Hampshire women with 46 years of service among them were fired, in part for gossiping and discussing rumors of an improper relationship between the town administrator and another employee that residents now agree were not true. You want to stay in the loop and not get hung by it.

Lisa Charles might have benefited from talking to her colleagues about their relationships with partners. If she learned which partners were reaching out to associates, she might have been able to make herself more available to them.

⇥ ⇤

Remember, your mentors do not necessarily have to look like you. Alexis Thomas,* an African-American woman, would never have made it through her first job in college without Jessica Siegel, a white Jewish woman. "I interned for a magazine and Jessica was the editor who basically adopted me as her office-child. She not only taught me about the administrative functionings of the office, but she also schooled me about the little things that I didn't understand about networking within the company. She explained the importance of going to social functions, especially the company holiday party. She took the time to explain the magazine business to me. She left me in charge of manning a display table at an exposition when she had to go out of town. She even introduced me to the internet. (Yes, this was quite a few years ago.) At the time, I took her kindness for granted and just assumed that all bosses were hands on. (Doesn't it seem like we had the best bosses earlier in life?)

"I actually looked forward to going to work each day because I knew that someone, Jessica, cared about my well-being. I cared about doing the best job possible, and this was a difficult feat. I wrote about computers and really technical, stiff and educational products. I was 19 years old and I wanted to write for this new hip-hop magazine called *Vibe*. Although I was bored out of my mind reading about the latest Microsoft products, the last thing I wanted to do was disappoint Jessica. During my 12-week summer internship, there was only one day that I did not report to work and that was due to a railroad strike. At the time, I didn't even think of the word mentoring, but that's exactly what she did for me. In return for Jessica caring about my career, she earned my loyalty."

⋯⇒◉ ◉⇐⋯

You should try to use all of your resources, from the secretary to a senior executive. People who have been with the organization for any length of time know the personality layout of your office and can advise you as to who is more affable and who is not. When you find a mentor, it's not necessary to call him or her a mentor. Some people get overwhelmed by titles and feel pressured to perform. To avoid the risk of someone shying away from helping you, just flow with the relationship. And most important, ask for help. When people know that you want to be mentored, the caring ones will work with you.

Here are some other strategies and approaches that professionals have used to move from outsider to insider.

⋯⇒◉ ◉⇐⋯

TAKING CHARGE: A WHITE WOMAN PARTNER IN HER LATE 30s SHARES HER STRATEGY FOR FINDING A MENTOR

"I have never really felt like an outsider in the workplace. I came to my firm because my former firm really did not have many women. So I knew that that was important for me and I wanted to work for and with a woman who was a rainmaker or whatever you want to call it. When I came to the firm, that person became my mentor and has always made sure, from my perspective, that I got the same work as everyone else and that I am accepted in every way. The mentoring has been very important, but the other thing is if I ever felt that I was not getting the same opportunities as someone else, I've always been very vocal about demanding what I think I'm entitled to. So, if a case came along and I thought that I was appropriate, I stood up and said that I was the appropriate person. With one partner in particular, that style works best with him. Once, a case came in and he was talking to me about it, or I had overheard him discussing who should staff it. I knew that it was going to be a high-profile case. I simply went to him and gave him my pitch as to why I was the appropriate person. And, I think whether I was the appropriate person or not really didn't matter. He was more impressed that I came forward and said I think I'm the right person.

"When I approach a partner, I am super prepared. I find that that is another thing that makes sure that you get the right work. As long as before you talk to someone you are super prepared, you have done the research, you've thought about your talking points and about what message you need to get across, you'll get the work."

⇢ᵺ ᵺ⇠

IT'S ALL ABOUT CONFIDENCE: A LATINO IVY LEAGUE GRADUATE DISCUSSES HIS INSIGHTS FOR LEVELING THE PLAYING FIELD

"I was fortunate enough to work in different environments where I was not subjected to bias. Oftentimes I was the 'first' within the respective groups to be a person of color and have a decent pedigree. So, I really didn't face exclusion. However, being in the executive search world, I hear from a lot of individuals that I provide counsel to that those challenges are clearly out there.

"There are always challenges, but not challenges based on

race or gender, but more so knowledge share. Behaviors are crucial in the marketplace. I provide counsel to many individuals.

"The mindset really predicates the behaviors. I was confident in what I was able to bring to the table. Why they hired me is really not predicated upon quotas or diversity programs but more so they hired me because I am a qualified individual. So entering into any type of work environment I know stepping into it that I was entitled to take on a specific role and while I was confident in my own self I think that I was able to project this outward. So those types of behaviors were not only being a risk taker and being proactive, but I think feeling a sense of confidence being myself and knowing that I can deliver. It sets the foundation. There are those who tend to be a little weak or meek and tend to be susceptible to attacks, whether they're founded or unfounded. There are those who always claim that they're a victim and within those who feel victimized there is a further dichotomy: those who are qualified, meaning those who are high performers, and those who are not high performers. So the question becomes, is the feeling of marginalization justifiable or not. So that's a separate issue unto itself.

"The advice I would give to individuals who may feel like Rudolph—that they don't get to play in any reindeer games—I would suggest that they get to know the political landscape. They have to be confident in who they are and what they bring to the table. If you're not going to be able to toot your horn, have others who will toot your horn. And be surrounded by individuals who are a good reflection of yourself. Find the mentor who is out there to help navigate the landmines that are in the corporate landscape. There is no magic bullet that provides the individual with that sense of comfort, but there are many tools that they can utilize to help minimize the phenomena of marginalization by virtue of your ethnicity or gender."

CHAPTER 2

LACK OF QUALITY
WORK ASSIGNMENTS
AND PROMOTIONS

We are a society driven by rewards. From the Olympic Games to most reality television shows, people will drive themselves to the limits of physical and mental endurance for the top prize. The same concept applies to the workplace.

What does the top prize look like in the workplace? Traditionally, it has meant a hefty paycheck and a corner office. However, Generations X and Y's work/life balance concept is rapidly changing what employees value and want out of their work environments. Today, people will barter a higher salary for leave and time away from the office. Sometimes we choose to work for organizations that pay less money in exchange for what we define as quality of life. However, we want the same compensation and recognition for our work as our majority colleagues receive for their work. When we are overlooked or denied opportunities that we know we deserve, we quickly lose interest in the organization and look for other opportunities. As Steven Levitt wrote in *Freakonomics: A Rogue Economist Explores the Hidden Side of Everything* (Harper Collins Publishers

Inc., 2005), "incentives are the cornerstone of modern life." Contrary to the popularly accepted notion that Generations X and Y are lazy, most of us shun stagnation. Generations X and Y want to contribute to organizations almost upon arrival. We want to feel as though the organizations we work for value our contributions and potential.

Women and people of color from Generations X and Y share many of their majority counterparts' feelings about the top prize in the workplace, but with more intensity. It is important to recognize that women and people of color, the two groups that are easiest to visibly identify as being under-represented in the workplace, were historically denied equal access to high-paying prestigious jobs. Today, we are taking advantage of the academic and workplace doors that have opened up to us. For example, as of 2006, 50% of law school graduates are women, 30% of business school graduates are women, and women outnumber male applicants to medical school. More people of color are graduating from high school and graduating from college than ever before. Given our his-tories of being denied equal opportunities in the workplace, it is twice as frustrating when we feel overlooked, underpaid, or prevented from contributing fully to the organization because of what we look like and not the quality of our work.

Just take a look at the investment banking industry. In a boston.com article, "Top Wall Street Jobs Still Elude Women, Minorities," Adam Klein, a partner at Outten & Golden LLP (and technically my former boss), explained, "There are sev-eral reasons why minorities and women may not see invest-ment banking as a good fit. For one, they may not get paid the same as their white male counterparts for doing the same job...These diversity efforts don't say anything about com-pensation. That's the bottom line issue." In the same article, Sharon Hadary, executive director of the Center for Women's

Business Research, told boston.com that, "[Women leave corporate careers for entrepreneurial ventures because] they didn't get an opportunity to influence the strategic direction of the organization, that no one listened to them." According to the article, women and people of color still have not pierced those managing director level and above senior positions that reap multimillion-dollar bonuses.

Whether it is investment banking, the entertainment industry, the government, a non-profit organization, or a law firm, the same concepts about equal pay, and more broadly equal treatment, apply. So, what are our incentives in the workplace? Based on conversations with young professionals from all backgrounds, incentives to work harder vary. It could be a promotion in title, a pay raise, a corner office, or challenging work assignments. In general, minorities in Generations X and Y want to feel as though we are making a difference in an organization and are recognized for our efforts.

PAY DISPARITIES

➺ ◦≡◦

When pay is our incentive, and there are disparities in the workplace and inequalities, we notice. Money is quantifiable and it is difficult to argue with numbers. For Ralph Georges,* standing up and demanding an explanation for the pay disparities in his workplace proved to be a liberating experience in more ways than he expected:

"By every indication, performance wise, I had done all sorts of strategic initiatives for the company. But when it came time for my bonus and my stock options, they weren't even year over year reflective of past performance which was good but not as good as the year I had done all these strategic initiatives.

The bonus was flat. Instead of being a 5% increase, it was a 4% increase. The stock options were less than the year before. I asked them to explain the logic in decreasing my compensation, my bonus, my merit increase and stock options.

"I did something I had never done before. I wrote a letter to my boss and my boss's boss and did a grid that showed the year over year difference in my bonus and my overall compensation and juxtaposed it against my performance—the things that I worked on where I got paid more than the most recent year where I worked on more strategic initiatives and launched products and got paid less. I was very straightforward. I wrote that, 'I was uncomfortable and I didn't think the bonus was acceptable based on a year to year comparison. I don't know how you got to this number. Please explain.' Here are the facts. Here is my work and my ratings. Tell me how we got here. And I did not leave it there. I said, not only do I need someone to give me a strong sense of how we got here but I would strongly suggest you reconsider.

"At this company you could formally put in a request for your bonus and even your ratings to be reviewed and reconsidered. So in my letter, I said I would like to understand my boss's thinking but I also would request for her to rethink the bonus and the increase given the facts that I posed. It takes a lot to formalize your concerns and appeal the decision and call into question the process and whether or not it's fair. So that was a big deal.

"A day went by and my boss told me that she felt sad that I felt as though I was treated unfairly. She agreed to take a look at my situation and look into it as soon as possible. During that time frame, coincidentally, I had been approached by a headhunter about another position. I started to think, maybe there is something better out there. Maybe this is a sign that I need to take. So I ended up negotiating a deal to leave to go to an entirely different kind of environment, an enterprising environment for more money and just a better deal. I left a number of years on the table at the company but I had this other opportunity that seemed compelling. There was a company that wanted to embrace me and my skills and experience and pay me more than I was making at the company I had been with for 10 years."

-->▣ ◼<--

LACK OF GROWTH OPPORTUNITIES

-->▣ ◼<--

For Nadine Lewis* the incentive was a promotion in title and responsibilities. Nadine was in her mid-twenties when she decided that she wanted to work for the public good. She joined a government agency with a class of other young attorneys who were willing to make financial sacrifices to pursue their interests in public service. As long as there were opportunities to grow professionally, they were fulfilled.

However, after a few years, Nadine came to the realization that her career was not going anywhere. She started with an entry-level title and after three years she still held the same entry-level title. According to her title, she was only capable of basic research and required heavy supervision. However, she had matured into the office's go-to attorney. When her supervisors wanted a case handled efficiently, they assigned her to it. There were even instances where her supervisors determined that she could handle cases better than the more senior attorneys.

While Nadine was pleased that her supervisors noticed her good work, she could not get over the promotion process. When she looked around the office, she noticed that no attorney had been promoted in seven years. Although she spent late nights at the office and handled the office's most complicated work, her request for a promotion in title was denied. Her supervisors were willing to give her a nominal bonus—they could not deny that she was a stellar performer—but they were not willing to tackle the bureaucracy involved with giving her a promotion. Her supervisors could not believe that she turned down their offer to give her more money, but that was in part because they didn't take the time to understand Nadine's incentives.

"I knew that my days with this government agency were numbered once I realized the limited opportunity for growth. To hold my position, I had to become a member of a union that had a collective bargaining agreement. My supervisor claimed that she could not promote me because of all the hoops she had to jump through with the collective bargaining agreement, but I felt like she was just playing the blame game. If she wanted to promote me she could have taken the time to initiate the promotion process. While more money would have been welcomed, I was more frightened that my skills would get dull and that I would become less marketable as time went by. My supervisors could not understand this. They often looked at my class as 'those young attorneys.' They didn't respect the fact that we had career aspirations. I knew that regardless of how many cases I tried, settled and mediated, future employers would always doubt my abilities if I still held an entry level title. I was not alone in deciding to leave. I joined the agency with seven other attorneys and when I left, only two remained. When I announced that I was leaving, the two attorneys who had not left yet asked me to keep an eye out for job opportunities. Who knew that even with an advanced degree there are dead-end jobs?"

⋯⧯ ⧯⋯

Ironically, too often minorities get advanced degrees to avoid working in a dead-end job but still find themselves stuck in a job where there are minimal opportunities for advancement.

⋯⧯ ⧯⋯

An African-American media executive friend of mine confided in me a time when he felt that his career was stalled. Although he earned an M.B.A. in marketing from a business school ranked in the top ten, he had the hardest time jumpstarting his career. "Part of my reason for leaving was based on disparities. The department had about 40 people and there were 3 blacks. I was the most senior black person. We were all treated as though we were not part of the company. I had made a decision after being there for a number of years, from a career standpoint, that I wanted to experience new things and develop a different set of experiences. I made a decision to post for another position within the company. I had received very good performance-related scores during my career but for whatever reason I could not break through and get the jobs I posted for. I was always the second runner-up or the first runner-up.

"Here's the thing that's crazy. I felt like there wasn't an opportunity to grow within my group. My group was so insular to the main body of the company that it did not allow me to bridge over to different career opportunities. I ended up being in a situation where there was no room to grow in the organization because I was not a part of the 'family.' It was a double-edged sword because not only was I not able to grow within the family, but there were a lot of businesses that did not feel that that organization was suitable as a launching pad for the bridge to other careers within the company. So it became almost like it was run like a separate entity, or almost like an agency. It made it difficult to find posts for positions. I told my boss and other people that I wanted to get more mainstream and find new opportunities within the broader company. I had been there for a number of years. Within a 6–9-month timeframe, I got no traction in any other positions. There was a real challenge that caused me to really rethink if I wanted to be there at all."

⇀⇢ ⇠⇤

Quality of Work Assignments

How projects are assigned is another source of feeling ostracized by the organization. Samira Hylton* tells a sobering story about how her supervisor sought to address the assignment process in her office when she brought the disparities to his attention. "I had a conversation with a partner about the quality of work that I was getting and the volume. I was not happy with the volume. I felt like it was too slow and I spoke with the partner about it. He comforted me by saying that it was a slow period for everyone but then he threw in a little piece of advice. He told me that I should try to get to know some of the senior associates because they were the ones that the partners know and they are who they'll work with. So, if I got to know the senior associates they would recommend me for assignments. Then he proceeded to name the associates and it was five or six white men who were in their early 30s. (At the time, I was a junior associate in my mid-20s.) These were guys who I felt like I had nothing in common with and the partner said I should get to know them informally. And I just wondered how I would go about doing that if it wasn't some sort of workplace thing. If I would just drop by their office and say, 'Hey, let's go have something to eat or let's hang out after work or what.' At that point I felt like that wasn't a realistic piece of advice for me."

Diversity of Work Assignments

Jocelyn Ade*, a transactional attorney in New York, was not so much concerned about the volume or quality of her work assignments. Instead her issue was the diversity of her work assignments. "My situation is unusual in the sense that I was on the same case for over four years. I needed to work on different matters. I needed to see cases from beginning to middle to end and I just wasn't getting that. There really wasn't much the firm could do other than letting me off the case or letting me see other types of work. After so many years you feel like you want a different experience. There are but so many years you can put in at the firm. I had done my time. I was getting to the point where I needed the additional experience. The firm tried to keep me, but I knew that I would not have been happy. I needed a more diversified, and varied portfolio of cases, or different clients and so on. I not only wanted corporate clients, but I wanted individual clients as well. At a bigger firm, you're more likely to have more corporate clients. In going to a smaller firm, you had a lot more individual clients. Smaller matters not worth too much, of course, come with their own risk as well. I wanted that experience as well.

"I left the second firm because it made promises to me about the type of work I would receive. I told them that I had only worked on larger cases and that I wanted to work on smaller cases. I was told that I would get a lot of smaller cases. While I was getting that, I was not getting to work on cases from beginning to end. I was just brought onto cases to finish up what other people had worked on."

→➡ ➡←-

CORPORATE GHETTOS

Quick question, in Corporate America, in which two departments do you find the most minorities? Usually, you find the most women and racial minorities in the mailroom and the cafeteria. Similar to noticing when we are a person in the minority, we also notice when minorities are in the majority when it comes to work assignments. Sadly, in corporate environments, often there is a direct inverse correlation between the desirability of a project and the percentage of women and racial minorities assigned to it: the less competitive the assignment, the higher the percentage of women and racial minorities staffed to the project.

⟶≈◎ ◎≈⟜

Bridgette Fox,* a Yale Law School graduate who worked in New York City as a corporate attorney, could not help but notice when select assignments were relegated to minorities in her firm. "There was an instance where I got assigned to work on a project where 90% of the people assigned to it were minorities. No one wanted to get stuck working on this project that was literally around the clock for six weeks straight. This was not a corporate project; it was a litigation project. I was not even doing the work that I was supposed to be doing. I remember there was a white male corporate associate, who was in the same year as me, who complained about it and was taken off the same day. All of the people pulled into the project, one after another, were Asian, Indian, and African-American. In that particular firm, I felt isolated because I was a person of color, not just because I was African-American.

"I did feel in different contexts and sometimes for different reasons that I was left out of things. I felt like I was never assigned the same level of work as non-minority associates. A couple of things that I remember, specifically, were where I spoke with a partner about the type of work I was assigned and that I was not getting assigned work. Was it something about me or my work product that wasn't good?

"We were assigned in units to various partners. I was in the Mergers and Acquisition (M&A) group, so there were two partners who had a handful of associates and they were supposed to assign work to them. In the group of associates, there were two racial minorities; there was an Asian fellow and me. I remember the partner saying that he had trouble getting work for me and the Asian guy. He couldn't really articulate any reasons for that. In my own feeling, I just thought well this is a person who simply doesn't want to assign work to minority associates. The two of us didn't have problem areas with our work. I knew that there were white males in the M&A group and they were getting a lot of work, good work. It made me feel pretty bad.

"This was a very new experience. For ten years before I went to law school I had been an executive at a large multinational commodities trading company and I had a lot of authority in that position. In my former field, the grains industry, which is very midwestern and white male dominated, there was at least a level of respect. I really didn't feel that when I got into this large law firm environment I would be obliterated because of the way I looked or people's assumptions about me. It was hard and that was one of the reasons why I left that firm after two years."

⇥ ⇤

ADVICE FOR MANAGERS

An employee's ability to grow depends on the quality of work and the level of responsibility given. If professionals are not challenged with new and exciting work, they often become bored and eventually will not become more valuable to the organization. Quality assignments and promotions usually go hand in hand. So, how does an organization limit the potential of some people getting better assignments, not because they cannot do the work but because they are unfairly perceived as being incapable.

Assignments should be business decisions instead of popularity contests. There should be a systematic assignment process where all employees are randomly in queue to get work on a rotating basis. Someone should be tasked each month to see what types of assignments the employees are receiving. If a manager gives an assignment out of queue, he or she should explain why. The manager should explain why he or she believes that an employee is not capable of handling an assignment. If a manager does not want to assign work to a person he or she deems is unqualified, the manager should make this known. Did the employee make a mistake the last time he or she worked on a similar assignment? Is this the employee's first time handling a particular assignment? The person managing assignments should have a mechanism in place to manage the situation to ensure that the employee does not spiral to the point where he or she is not trusted with competitive assignments and becomes useless to the organization. Close review of each employee gives the organization a better opportunity to intervene early and determine how to bring the underperforming employee up to speed. This way the organization can cure a talent issue before it becomes a potential dilemma.

If an employee is truly not performing well, from the first instance, let the employee know. As the employee, I could never understand the chicken-hearted attempts supervisors made to avoid situations. I always thought that since the supervisor was in control, he or she would take control. However, that was usually not the case. My colleagues and I experienced supervisors who took circuitous routes around addressing situations, such as punctuality, writing abilities, organization or ability to effectively meet deadlines. It was as though they wanted to avoid any hurt feelings but in reality they were allowing a bad situation to fester. Avoiding performance issues is like leaving an old and dirty adhesive bandage on a wound. While it's better to peel off the bandage and avoid infection, many supervisors fear the sting of removing the bandage and would rather cause an infection. You are potentially damaging the employee's career if you don't act immediately.

Senior management should also be made aware of the importance of looking beyond the employee's façade and instead valuing his or her work. In my employment education seminars, I often hear managers explain that they may give more work to one employee as opposed to another because of personal likes or dislikes. Once a manager even told me that he would avoid working with an employee if he didn't have anything in common with the employee. He admitted that he wouldn't invite the employee he didn't like for personal reasons to strategy meetings or include the employee in any assignments that involved heavy interaction. I would not let the manager off the hook by merely accepting his personal dislike for an employee as a justification for not giving him or her assignments. I wanted to know what did the employee do for you to dislike him or her? Did the employee offend you? If so, did you address it? Did the employee submit shoddy work? If so, did you address it? Because, until supervisors truly confront their preferences for working with one person over another, supervisors may be subconsciously harboring bias, assumptions, and stereotypes about an employee. If supervisors have a preference for only working with people who look, act and sound like them, they are unfairly denying all of their other employees an equal opportunity to advance within the organization and are undercutting the organization's diversity efforts.

ADVICE FOR PROFESSIONALS AND STUDENTS

Professionals in the minority should also have a strategic plan for growth. Find a trusted advisor, and have him or her help you to map milestones for your career. This will help you to know if you are getting the quality and quantity of work to achieve your end goals. If you're not reaching your milestones, you will know sooner rather than later if your organization is doing enough to develop your skills. If it is not, then you can take proactive steps to improve the situation.

If you feel as though your primary work responsibilities are not giving you the challenges you want, be creative in finding other ways to enhance your skills. Volunteer projects for community and professional trade associations are a good way to build your management skills. For lawyers, pro bono projects are a good way to get exposure to a practice area and may even offer the opportunity to develop your leadership and management skills. Plus, since most organizations are grateful for your assistance, many will give you the training and guidance that you may not get in your work environment. Although it might be unpaid work, it is still resume-building work.

In 2005, the *New York Times* did a piece about how 41% of minority women gained leadership skills through volunteer work with their church or community organization yet this leadership never translated into the workplace. Depending on your relationship with your manager, you may want to consider inviting him or her to an event that you have organized so that you can show off your management skills. An approach may involve *casually* telling your manager about the event or accomplishment. If you were recognized by your church or a civic organization, you should think about putting the award in your office. Awards spark curiosity and your manager will most likely inquire about your award. If you really feel as though your manager would not care to know about your involvements outside of work that demonstrate valuable workplace leadership skills, you should strongly consider whether you are working in an environment that is right for you.

Apart from developing leadership skills, volunteer work gives you the freedom to try new things. You can work in a substantive area completely different from what your position offers. For instance, I always had an interest in learning about negotiating sponsorships with corporations because I wanted to increase my fundraising skills. As a practicing attorney, I never had the opportunity in my day-to-day work to draft sponsorship forms. However, while serving on the National Association for Multi-Ethnicity in Communication's Programming Board, I was constantly trying to find new ways to generate funding for programs. I learned how to create sponsorship letters, media kits, and other public relations tools to get funding. Today, I use these skills on a daily basis operating my business and non-profit organization.

Ultimately, the most effective strategy for advancing within an organization is to consistently churn out quality work, obviously. The following young attorney has a fool-proof strategy for overcoming, and staving off, being overlooked:

STAYING A FEW STEPS AHEAD OF MANAGEMENT

Clients have a tendency to forum shop to avoid working with me. I am the only female person of color in my group. I've actually indicated to my management that I can only be useful if they copy me on responses or tell clients that I will be the one responding because I am the point of contact. So I've taken that direct approach. To certain degrees this has worked. But I still think that it's human nature for my supervisors to think, "I'll just handle it." Or, "I can handle it quicker." And nine times out of ten that's not accurate because they don't know all the details of the matter. If you are one step or two steps ahead of management, they're not going to know everything.

You should know information like the back of your hand. You want to make yourself more indispensable than most.

Sometimes another way in which you may feel under-valued is being underpaid. If you suspect that you are being underpaid, you should research the issue before you take any action. There are a number of websites like Salary.com where you can compile salary information about your industry, cross-referenced with information about your level of experience. After this information is gathered, the last thing you want to do, though, is complain about not making as much money as the person sitting in the office next to yours. Your plan now needs to turn into a negotiation strategy. Ron Shapiro, author of *The Power of Nice* and agent to major league baseball players and famous personalities, told me about his simple, but com-prehensive approach to negotiations: Prepare, Probe and Pro-pose. Ask questions about your salary and listen to your boss's reasons for his salary determination. Once you have prepared and probed, think about proposals that will meet your and the organization's needs. Feel free to offer creative, but reason-able, solutions to resolve the salary gap. Aside from asking for the obvious—more money—consider proposing solutions that will enhance your quality of life: additional leave; promotion in title; flex-time that allows you to arrive and leave at times that work best for you and the company; bonus; and other similar benefits.

You may also consider working with a headhunter or pro-fessional placement recruiter. Since companies are constantly contacting temporary placement agencies to fill positions, these professional recruiters know the employment market. A headhunter can assist you with your job hunt, polish your resume, and tell you how much your position is worth in the open market. To find a reputable headhunter, ask your col-leagues and trusted advisors for a referral. It is always best to work with someone whose work is familiar to someone you trust.

To avoid becoming extinct to your organization, you should look for opportunities to sharpen your skills. This may involve taking courses, reading articles, and even writing articles about your area of business. Public Enemy's Chuck D, one of the most politically conscious rappers from the 1980s and 1990s, summarized how important it is to stay ahead of the curve:

ONE SHOW PONY: DIVERSIFYING YOUR SKILLS SET

Young minority professionals should come into the situation where they're told that they can add diversity, then they have to look inside themselves and be diverse inside themselves. I mean that you can't come in there (and this is an unwritten rule for minorities) less equipped and with less drive than everybody else. You can't come in being a one-trick pony, being a master of just one trade. Immediately your entire department or your particular niche could be wiped away with just the stroke of a pen. So it pays to be very well schooled in all aspects of whatever business that you're trying to get into, especially when you're going into a corporation. The more things that you happen to be privy to, the more positions that you may be able to fill. There are times when your aim for a particular position happens to not be there because it's a game of numbers, a game of racism, or just the good old fashioned game of saying that you're underqualified.

CHAPTER 3

PERCEIVED UNDERPERFORMANCE

We all have a way we want things done. We have our own styles, and often we would prefer that others who work for us adopt them. Diversity includes accepting different work styles. It means looking beyond a regimented way of working and understanding that the work will get done, just differently. When our work style is in the minority, we are often victims of unnecessary scrutiny where managers will search for flaws in our work.

For instance, in the early days of telecommuting, many managers resisted the trend out of fear that they would not be able to closely monitor their employees. Much of the telecommuting debate revolved around managers' work preferences and demanding face time with employees. There were numerous articles written about managers who did not believe that their employees were capable of maintaining a high-level of performance if they worked from home. Today, organizations realize that in order to remain competitive, they have to meet their employees' work needs halfway. Gone are the days where face time is necessary to complete a project. With mobile devices, laptops, and other technology to keep employees connected to the office, an employee can accomplish as much at home as in the office.

Similar to how work styles can obscure a manager's perceptions about an employee's abilities, visible characteristics can also distract managers from truly valuing the employee's work. Sometimes those in the minority might not be appreciated because their managers and co-workers are considering the *person* doing the work and not the *content*. When our subjective perception about how someone will work interferes with their objective performance, everyone loses. The employee perceived as underperforming constantly has to waste time fighting to defend his or her reputation, and the culprits risk ruining the organization's reputation for being a healthy and productive place to work. While I'm sure that some of the companies that appear in *Fortune* magazine's yearly list of the "Top 100 Companies to Work For" are led by managers who are real tyrants, I'm certain that the companies with a critical mass—and reputation—of employees complaining about bad bosses did not make the list.

⇝ ⇜

When Carolina Lopez* spoke with me to discuss the types of behaviors that ushered her out of her first law firm, I knew that I was in for a good story when she got up to close the door. Carolina's resilience in the face of being undervalued for her contributions was an experience that only the strong could survive. "In my prior employment with a big New York firm with a small Los Angeles office I felt excluded. It's hard to tell you the exact reason, but I'm convinced it was because I was young, I was female, and Latina.

"I was assigned to work with a particular partner and a

mid-level associate. They had a team approach on some of their matters and in this particular situation that's what happened. The partner and I got along really well to the point where I think that the mid-level associate felt a little bit uncomfortable and threatened or something. I don't know what it was. She was a white female. The partner was a white male. He was a little bit older, and she was older than I was. (She came to the law as a second career.) I had done some pretty good work and had gotten some good feedback. We were working on something and I got excluded from discussions between the partner and the mid-level associate on a matter I was intimately involved in and had done a lot of the work on. Then, I had done a written assignment and was specifically told that she wanted to meet with me and give me feedback where she then proceeded to lambaste me, indicating that I didn't know how to write. This really happened. She told me that I didn't know how to write, that I didn't know how to grammatically put together a correct sentence, and that she was convinced that I learned to write English as a second language.

"This was the most humiliating, embarrassing moment that I could ever imagine and it prompted me to shortly leave the firm. I did end up talking to the partner about this particular project. His view of my work was completely and dramatically different. So, it was one of those experiences where I'm convinced that she acted the way she acted number one because of my gender and also because she knew about my ethnic background. She proceeded to try to press buttons that would maybe resonate with me or make me feel that I was not worthy or competent. Questioning my ability to write English—it was just an incredible experience. To this day when I've run into her at court, I can barely look at her. She knows full well what happened. I don't know if many people got wind of what occurred. I don't know how many people I shared it with but I certainly did not feel that this was a place where I could continue to work given what occurred. I have to be honest; it really affected my self-esteem for a little while. It was just the most incredible thing that had ever happened to me. What was crazy was that I had gotten some wonderful feedback prior to and subsequent to the incident from the partner. So I knew that I didn't have trouble with my writing or anything. It was really just an attempt to make me think that I was inadequate or maybe to try to get rid of me. I don't know. I couldn't tell you exactly what was going on. The experience is still fresh in my mind. I started to question even the basics. After I got out of that firm, that mid-level associate ended up leaving the firm maybe a year or so after, and then got divorced. This person had some problems.

"The whole experience was incredibly negative but I think I got some good out of it in realizing that I need to take ownership and mentor, especially women of color, which is what I've been very committed to in the profession over the last several years. I don't know if you know this but I'm the hiring partner for my firm. Every mentee that I've had has been a woman of color. I've hired mostly women, but not all. I've increased our numbers and our racial and ethnic diversity in the firm. What I'm saying is that this event, but not just this event but my life experiences, prompted me to take steps to try to prevent this from happening in my immediate world in the future."

⟶ ⟵

Nathan Jones* never had to wonder what his superiors thought about him; they blatantly told him that they didn't think that he had the mental aptitude for engineering. Nathan, an African-American man in his 20s, joined the military a few years after the Army's advertising campaign of "Be All that You Can Be." He comes from a hardworking family from North Carolina and he had the potential of being the first in his family to even consider college. Unfortunately, his unfamiliarity with the college application and financial aid process convinced him that he could not afford college. That's when he turned to the U.S. Navy. He entered a competitive engineering program and was determined to make the most of his military career.

Soon after he joined this elite program, he quickly learned that the military was integrated but not yet equal. "One instance where I felt like an outsider was in the military when my superiors made an obvious attempt to get rid of me because of my race. In the nuclear power program while you were often tested there were not many instances where one's knowledge was tested outside of scheduled tests. These instances—Academic Boards (ACs)—were dreaded by the students and reserved for those who had demonstrated a real deficiency. All of a sudden, the officers came up with an opportunity to randomly test five students' knowledge of where they were in the program. The day before the test, it somehow became a test of one person's knowledge. Me. When I was chosen for the AC there was one other black guy in my class of 30 people; initially he was also *randomly* selected to take the test.

"Before taking the test, I had to spend time interviewing with the officer who had set this whole thing in place. The officer made it clear in our interview that he thought that I would not pass the test, and I disagreed with him. He explained that people such as me did not belong in the program. He explained that people like me were better at other things, such as basketball and physical things. It was thinly veiled but what he was referring to was still there. In an instance like that you feel like an outsider because it is being made clear you that are an outsider.

"Although I had already qualified to be in the nuclear program, it's like they were giving me an extra test to see if I qualified to be in the program. You have to qualify to get to each stage in the program. At prototype you go through the in-class stage where they teach you everything you're supposed to know to get to the next stage, e.g., operation of the plant, in-hull. At that point if you show that you can't keep up, then they start testing you.

"At the time, I was in prototype, which was the third phase to becoming a fully qualified nuclear operator. I was still in the training phase. There was nothing that I could think of that prompted the officers to test me. It started out supposedly as a random thing. If it was truly random, the decision to test five students could not have been prompted by anything the students had done. If we believe in the random quality of this decision to test then it does not matter what I had or had not done anyway. It was just too coincidental how it went from completely random — testing five students—to selecting one person.

"The other thing making it clear that there was an attempt to get rid of me was that when these ACs are conducted, they were usually 10 to 30 minutes in length. The majority of people who took them failed. The longest ACs were close to an hour. My AC board, which I would venture to say there is no record of, was eight hours long, which was the longest in the history of the program. An eight-hour AC board guaranteed you were going to fail. I didn't fail though.

"The way I operate—assuming that they really wanted to get rid of me because of my race—caused me to want to be there even more, specifically to do two things. One, to show that while you may think that people like me can't do, yes we can. And two, because of the constraints of the military and the way you can get back at people, I thought that this officer must be a racist so my mission, as long as I was there, was to qualify for the next phase as early as possible, so that I could choose when I stood watch and find this officer and stand watch with him. I knew it would drive him crazy, which is what I did. There was very little that I could do to him, but there's nothing that he could do to me once I qualified. He had to look at me every time we stood watch.

It was the military, so I had to stay with the program. To get out of that program, one of two things usually happen, either you have a mental condition from the stress or you are going to be dishonorably discharged— you don't normally just switch programs; they have invested too much in you.

"I did not re-enlist and I am no longer in the military. You can make a heck of a lot more money in nuclear power outside of the military and you don't have to deal with the same type of stress. Plus, as a black man it is difficult to be in such a white program with such a white view and feel as though you can remain true to yourself. For me the decision to leave rested as much in my need not to feel dependent on the military as it did in the fact that I could not do as I had seen other black men do: go along to get along."

⟜⟜ ⟜⟜

Tammy Ellis* had a similar experience where her supervisor determined that she did not have the intellectual aptitude to do her job. Tammy is one of those people who thinks quickly and chooses her words very carefully. Whether she is in a conversation with her girlfriends or is giving a presentation to attract a multimillion-dollar client, she is engaging. Although it is painfully obvious how eloquent and intelligent Tammy is, her employer could not see beyond her dark chocolate complexion to appreciate her talent. "When I first started my practice after law school, I wanted to be a tax attorney. And for the first eight months of practice I was in the tax department in a large law firm. As I found out as I started practicing, the department that I was in was very typical of New York tax departments in that I was one of seven females in a 23-person department. I was the only black person, and one of four non-Jews.

"The bulk of the Jewish practitioners in the department were orthodox and male. That surprisingly turned out to be a very exclusionary experience for me in that oftentimes people spoke in Yiddish to my exclusion. There was very strong, reasonably so I guess—although uncomfortable to me—very pro-Israel sentiment and people were very willing to speak about their political and religious beliefs very freely, very openly and with the assumption that everyone else in the room agreed. As one of the few non-Jews, I was always the one who didn't order the kosher meal where typically people who want kosher meals are the exception. For me, it was the complete opposite.

"I also felt that that was the toughest professional experience because I also felt that I was targeted by one of the partners. I don't really know what his reasoning for it was but much of his criticism were things like, 'I don't think that you have the mental intellect to do this type of work,' which was very surprising to me because I definitely have academic degrees and work experience that show otherwise. It was the first time that I had someone say to me, not that I didn't do a good job, but they didn't think that I had the ability to learn something, which was very disheartening and was very unjustified. And what substantiated to me that it was unjustified was that at one point I was working on a project with this partner and another partner. They were both supervising me. When I went to the partner who was very critical of me, he always had negative comments about what I was doing. And then I would go to the other partner, and he would say how excellent my work was and how much ahead of what he expected I would have done as a first year. So, it just seemed like such a dichotomy between the two opinions.

"And even when the project was a presentation to be given to the department I got tons of accolades from the people who attended the presentation, yet this partner refused to acknowl-edge that it was a well-reasoned, well-thought-out, provocative presentation for whatever reason. And so, being that he was a partner he made it very difficult for me because of course there would be partnership discussions and I was not there to defend myself and he just made very negative comments about me to even the partners that I didn't work with.

"While it could be said that maybe that's just the way he was with junior people, my officemate who was an orthodox Jewish male and junior in the firm was idolized by this part-ner. Even where we had very similar assignments where I got chastised for not knowing something, my officemate was taken under his wing. Even when my officemate made mistakes the partner acted as though it was to be expected. My officemate got a lot of breaks and coddling that I did not get and I could not understand for what reason, other than the fact that I was not a Jewish male or someone that this partner felt comfortable with.

"So towards the end I finally decided to leave the depart-ment because I refused to put myself through that situation any longer. Because I had good relationships with other people in the firm and other partners in the firm, I was able to get out of that department and into the corporate department where I was much more successful than I would have been had I continued to fight the system in the tax department."

→═ ═←

ADVICE FOR MANAGERS

Sometimes professionals in the minority are not given an equal opportunity to succeed in the workplace even though most organizations have "Equal Employment Opportunity (EEO)" statements on their websites and within their marketing materials. In fact, the professionals I interviewed for this section all worked for organizations that have chief diversity officers, affinity groups, and well-publicized diversity principles, or advertise in magazines and other media that are marketed to minorities. While EEO policies are important to recruiting purposes, they are even more powerful to current employees. Equal opportunity practices make it possible for employees who are underrepresented in the workplace to know that their work is not in vain, and that it is possible for them to advance within the organization. When we are treated fairly, we know that we are taken seriously and are valued by those with whom we work.

Each year, organizations spend millions of dollars on diversity training and programs; however, what use is training if the practices are not implemented? The resources expended on diversity efforts appear to be a waste of money and time if supervisors are not willing to give all employees a fair opportunity to churn out quality work.

To ensure that supervisors are using a consistent benchmark of performance when evaluating majority and underrepresented employees, they should be asked to describe what standards they used to evaluate their employees' work. When a supervisor complains about a person's work, the supervisor should be required to explain, in detail, exactly how that person's work was inadequate. What set of metrics were used to measure the employee's work? What could the employee have done better or differently? Are you judging this employee by the same standards used to evaluate the other employees with the same years of experience and seniority? These are essential questions for ensuring fairness when evaluating an employee's work. In short, supervisors should have objective criteria for evaluating an employee's work.

Organizations should not be afraid to be courageous and

take bold moves if they are serious about creating and fostering diversity. An organization's leadership cannot be afraid to stand up to managers who have the ability to taint the experiences of professionals in the minority. Managers should be made aware of how they are not meeting the organization's diversity goals and should be reminded of how this failure is going to affect the company's business. Remember those feelings of being a person in the minority and feeling as though you didn't belong? Eventually when people tell you enough times through their actions that you don't belong, you may start to believe it. Similarly, talented professionals who are constantly under-recognized and underestimated will not stay where they are treated as though they are not wanted. Managers should be evaluated by their subordinates to truly get a sense of how their conduct is perceived, and these evaluations should be taken seriously.

ADVICE FOR PROFESSIONALS AND STUDENTS

The best advice I can offer as a former employment law attorney is to watch for signs of disparities. Often, my clients would have perfect 20/20 hindsight about issues that seemed trivial and snowballed into nightmares. They would tell me about the early stages of a plot to sabotage their career, yet they overlooked the signs. They didn't take it too seriously when the manager strictly enforced the office's policies when it applied to them but then ignored the same policy when another employee was involved. They were the only person whose work was excessively criticized but they received the least support and coaching. They had the most work piled on them. They did not get upset when a manager made an offensive joke and comment that offended them. It was not until employees were fired or denied a bonus that the employees got upset and found meaning in these events.

Your work is your brand and you can not afford to have someone tarnish it. Too many times, my clients would present a file filled with positive evaluations but were still fired because someone did not like them for personal reasons and used workplace leverage to squeeze them out of the organization. The previous testimonials are clear examples of how managers' subjective and personal beliefs can taint the workplace dynamic. Tammy, Carolina, and Nathan were not people who objectively underperformed. They were commended for their work by some and admonished by others who were out to sabotage. Take note (or actually tons of notes for your records) when you feel that someone is unfairly disparaging your work or your performance.

Remember, people talk and you want everyone to say good things about you. Once you locate the source of the negative comments about your work, be sure to address them and clear up any misperceptions about your performance. Maybe someone mistakenly thought that you missed a deadline, when you were actually ahead of schedule. You should try to set things straight. Try to find the right time to address the source of the negative comments. Often speaking to this person alone and during a slower work period is more effective than addressing the person in a group during the office's busy season. If you are concerned about what you should say, practice your talking points with a trusted senior advisor. Remember to make the most of the people who care about your career.

When you get written accolades for your work, be sure to collect them. In your personal positive evaluations file you should also keep any emails that you receive about your good work. Not only do positive emails cheer you up on those down days, they also create the record you may one day need to defend your work or file a complaint against the company.

CHAPTER 4

INSENSITIVITY

Often insensitivity is caused by arrogance and a feeling that as management or a person in the majority, it's good to be the king and that they can do or say as they please. In other instances, insensitivity is the result of ignorance and not knowing or being aware of how your words and actions offend the next person. In either situation, insensitivity still hurts. Insensitivity is not only the failure to care about others' feelings or circumstances but is also the lack of responsiveness. The person who ignores complaints of insensitive conduct is just as guilty as the person who makes the offending comment or gesture. The failure to do or say the right thing permeates all workplace relationships and fosters a culture in which insensitivity is deemed acceptable. When a co-worker or manager creates an environment that is uncomfortable or hostile, it just makes going to work more difficult. It becomes a draining experience to have someone belittle you and chip away at your self-esteem.

While cultural insensitivity is the most common form of

insensitivity that makes people feel excluded within an organization, callous behavior can take all shapes and forms. It could be fat jokes, unflattering comments about someone's color, or rude statements about someone's socioeconomic background. Although the law maintains a "reasonable standard" for determining legally actionable conduct and lists the protected categories for prohibited insensitive conduct, people are still offended regardless of whether they are entitled to have their day in court.

When I spoke with Baby Boomers about whether they encountered insensitivity in the workplace, they all said yes; however, most did not realize it at the time. Many felt as though their majority counterparts did not really understand them and excused them for saying and doing stupid things. Others felt that insensitive banter was par for the course as a minority. As long as their jobs were secure, they did not get too upset about the "silly" things the guy in the cubicle next to them would say and do.

➛═ ═◄

Jose Ramirez's* experience is a good example of how a Boomer didn't even recognize how detrimental jokes about his ethnicity were to his career and how he missed the signs that he was an outsider. "I've only had one time in my career that I felt like an outsider, and I didn't realize that I was feeling that way until I got much older and that particular part of my career was behind me. I am Hispanic and I realize now what was going on probably had to do with a bias. This happened earlier in my career. I had just gotten back from Vietnam, so that puts me in my mid-twenties. I worked for a company that was involved with mining. I felt that it was more that I was young or possibly I didn't have the right training or the right background. But then I realized that my peers, who were not much different than I was in terms of their backgrounds, seemingly were moving along professionally much quicker than I was. Their progress was better. I got to thinking about questions that bother me now but didn't bother me then. There was a guy who was in the position to promote me who would insert 'humorous' jokes about me being Spanish. Again, I was born in this country. I come from a Cuban background. I wasn't thinking prejudice at that point. I wasn't thinking bias at that point. Now as I get older, I realize that that could have been the case.

"The sad part of the story is that I was with the company for 12 years. If my feelings are correct, my ethnicity made it more difficult to advance more quickly within the company than if I had realized that that was the problem. I'm assuming my ethnicity was the problem."

⟶⟩⟩ ⟨⟨⟵

Minorities from Generations X and Y are much more astute at detecting and recognizing insensitivity from their managers and co-workers. We realize that jokes are not just fun and play and tell a lot about what a person really feels. Going one step further, we understand that the same emotions that fueled a racist joke could also fuel the decision to deny us a promotion or even fire us.

⟶⟩⟩ ⟨⟨⟵

In a sharp contrast to our parents, we not only recognize discrimination masked in insensitive conduct but we also take immediate action. Victor Chen* was known for laughing on the outside at insensitive Asian jokes, but his colleagues had no idea to what extent he strategized on the inside. Victor worked in the financial services industry for a few years after graduating from college, believing that there was real equality and equal opportunity. Instead, he met racism against Asians cloaked in frat boy humor. "Here's the interesting thing, one of my co-workers was being made fun of. He was Vietnamese and he had a somewhat striking resemblance (more or less) to Kobayashi, the hot dog–eating champion. His Asian-ness was used as a comical jump-off point for the predominantly Caucasian males in the group. His accent was also made fun of. It wasn't blatant like, 'Oh, he's from Vietnam and he eats dogs.' It was always like, 'Oh, he has a funny accent. Look at the things he does. He's very thrifty.' The composite of it was a very subtle, 'Oh he's other. He's different. He's good at *that*, he's so focused.' It was very subtle, like 'Oh, this is what John* is good for.' No one said that because he's Vietnamese he's this way, but it was almost like, and I perceived, that the message was, 'John's never going to be a manager. He's really good at what he does and we really appreciate him for that.'

"And I spoke about this with—aside from John—the other Asian-American male in my group. The conversations were very much about 'they won't look out for us. We need to do what's best for us to get the best out of the situation.' At the end of the day, our own self-interests were a priority while we were working there. We were finding a way to fit in, but knowing that we would never exactly fit in. I played the game.

"I just worked really hard and I did a good job. I ascended to a place in that team where I did such a large volume of work and I had such a wide body of knowledge that I really became indispensable. So to me it became about work ethic and not worrying about marginalization. My goal was not to ascend and become a manager there. My goal was to get my bills paid and do some interesting work before I found the next big thing. When I found the better thing, I made the change to a career that I was more passionate about."

⇥ ⇤

Victor's situation is typical. Managers and employees receive extensive EEO compliance training and know how to avoid obvious and blatant acts of discrimination. However, just as quickly as they have found subtle ways to marginalize minority employees, we have found ways to decode their behavior.

Heidi Williams is proud to be openly gay and openly identified in this book. She repeatedly found herself in that uncomfortable situation where the people around her revealed their true thoughts and feelings about lesbians before they learned about her sexual orientation. "I can share some experiences I had when I was a flight attendant, which was an interesting job because you don't go to work with the same people everyday. Every other job experience I've had you develop a rapport and people get to know you. The airline industry is unique in that each time you go on a trip you could fly with different people and you could never fly with the same person twice. So you have to develop a relationship with people on each flight.

"On trips, whether it was one day, two days, or five days of working with those same people, there were numerous times that I would be on a trip and be enjoying the flight attendants' company. We would talk about whatever things we had in common—what books we recently read, that we both were runners, anything. And it never occurred to me to bring up my sexual orientation. I'm a lesbian. They didn't bring up their sexual orientation so I would not bring up mine. It would not be something that I hid, but it just would not come up. Then when I thought I was really getting along with someone and had established a really good rapport, all of a sudden they would make a really homophobic comment. Unfortunately, I would feel really paralyzed. I think it was because it would catch me off guard.

There was a time when I flew with a woman I just met. I was training for a marathon at the time and we happened to talk about how we were both runners, and we were talking about the books that we were reading. I really thought we were enjoying working together. On day three of this trip, she came and looked at me with disgust and said, 'Oh my God, did you see how many dykes are on this flight?' It just took me off guard. I literally could not say anything. I think that whatever the stereotypes are, I fit into the 'normal' appearance for a woman, whatever that means. People assume that I am straight. Unfortunately, they share their prejudices and bigotry with me and think that I will agree with them and don't realize that I'm part of the group they're talking about.

"When I was a flight attendant I would hear these negative remarks and I thought it was really interesting because my roommate, who was also a flight attendant and was a gay man, did not encounter the same degree of public homophobia. He was rather effeminate and I believe that there is a stereotype that male flight attendants are gay and some of them are. I think that people didn't make comments around him because they just assumed.

"I started to out myself before people could make the negative comments. I would put rainbow stickers on my name badge and on my bag. I certainly attempted to bring things up in a conversation as early as possible. Unfortunately, a lot of people don't know that the rainbow sticker stands for diversity and has been adopted as a symbol of gay pride and so it didn't always work. I think that at this point in life, I would feel disappointed in myself for not feeling like I immediately had the courage to say something back. I think over the years I've changed and attempted to immediately speak up so that I don't feel like so much of my power has been taken away. I'm really comfortable with and proud of who I am.

"I actually got laid off after September 11th and by the time the airline called me back I had another career. It was really fun to fly around for four years for free but I was ready for something more meaningful. I have moved on to a career as a full-time activist fighting for equality and I find this work extremely rewarding."

⟐ ⟐

With increased EEO compliance programming, public tolerance and the political correctness movement, so much of today's insensitivity is subtle. Although Heidi's co-workers thought they were safe to bash homosexuality when they were talking to Heidi, they had no idea that they were offending her.

⟐ ⟐

June Maples* was not naïve when her colleagues and superiors erected communication barriers to exclude her from conversations and business in general.

"I did not share in the common ethnicity and culture of the majority of the department. I was a black woman and I wasn't Jewish. I was outspoken, but a personable person in that I could carry on conversations with people in the department as well as with people outside of the department. Oftentimes during meetings—be they small meetings with two or three people where assignments were given—or be they larger department meetings, people started talking about things in Yiddish in front of me. In my opinion it was just done purposely to exclude me because I don't speak Yiddish and I didn't understand what they were talking about. As a woman of Afro-Caribbean descent I could not become a part of these conversations and it became exclusionary."

June may have been in the room during many conversations with her superiors, but she was kept out of the conversation.

Basically, she was invited to the party but she was not asked to dance.

⊸⊫⊚   ⊚⊫⊸

At the risk of doling out common sense, when people are forced to internalize offensive comments and behavior in the workplace as a coping mechanism, it can affect their ability to think and work productively.

⊸⊫⊚   ⊚⊫⊸

Sometimes It's What Was Said and How It Was Said

Gem Winehouse*, an advertising sales representative for a global media company, spends unnecessary amounts of time thinking about what she says because of a mistake she made earlier in her career. "I was in a sales meeting of about 10 people and I accidentally said 'pacific' instead of 'specific.' My white female boss at the time said to me in front of the group, 'We don't speak Ebonics at the office, we speak proper English.' My colleagues gasped when our boss said this. Now, the California Ebonics debate was being covered at that time in the news so my boss probably just labeled all black speech as Ebonics or black slang. However, I was still insulted and told my boss that my saying 'pacific' instead of 'specific' had nothing to do with Ebonics."

⊸⊫⊚   ⊚⊫⊸

Gem was frustrated that her mistake was no longer an individual's mishap but it was now intrinsic of her race because her boss determined that all blacks speak Ebonics. This type of generalizing and negative stereotyping about employees does not go unnoticed.

Subash Singh* has had her fair share of feeling frustrated because of insensitive ethnic stereotypes. "There was an attorneys' meeting where one of the senior partners made a comment about people whose last names were not American, and specifically she enumerated that they were Chinese, Indian, and Korean last names. And, she made a comment about how these individuals, once they got their degrees from US colleges, were going to go back to their home countries. So that definitely was amazing to me because I have an Asian-sounding last name. I'm sitting across from the woman and am literally rendered invisible. On two levels it was troublesome: one, I wondered, 'Is that how you think of me? A non-American or a foreigner?' The second was the partner's refusal to see me as having any race or identity and just whitewashing me in her eyes.

"I've talked among my peers about it but I have not directly confronted anyone who has said something or made me feel uncomfortable. I've talked to two other senior people about the foreigner comment and they agreed it was inappropriate and they couldn't believe it was said. Their reaction was she just didn't realize what she was saying, which does not justify the situation. These senior people asked if I wanted to speak to her about it. They tried to think of ways of addressing the issue whether it involved me personally or other people stepping up and saying something.

"Aside from that, when I first started working for my firm, and it still continues, Caucasians are far more comfortable interacting with each other—whether it's talking in the kitchen or going down the hall and just saying hi to people. I just find that it's easier for them to banter about and I've noticed that these people avoid my eye if I'm walking down the hall and they are not at ease; I've been here 2 ½ years. You would think that I've gotten over that. It's kind of hard because there are not many other comparators—that is, other people of color—so it becomes hard to see whether it's just me. I've spoken to another colleague of color and she has expressed similar concerns and experiences where one or two people are unable to have conversations with her but have no problem being relaxed and chummy around other associates our age and career level. This happens with the administrative staff and partners.

"It makes me less invested in the place. It becomes more like a job as opposed to a career. It is a smaller office and people who have been here longer know much more about each other. I don't feel some kind of bond or camaraderie on that level. It makes me very angry. It's a kind of anger that the other associate of color and I have talked about. It's very frustrating. Generally, if you are in the minority and you are in a place where such incidents happen, whether it's overt comments or more subtle interactions with other people, if you raise concerns and say, 'I think this is problematic' or 'I can't believe you said that,' the people you are trying to confront get very defensive. Their response is that you have no right to anger if you feel offended or excluded as a minority. You have no right to that level of emotion because inevitably the people whom you are talking to and are trying to correct or point out their behavior or their words, they are going to shut down. The only way, apparently, to reach the people in the majority who are making these comments or acting in such a manner is if you can be nice. It gets very aggravating.

"I have checked in with my peers. It seems like the other associates, when I've talked to them, by and large have the same reaction like, 'Oh my God, I can't believe that just happened.' But then it becomes apparent that at the partner level—and this is where I wonder if it is a generational thing—they are just not as self-aware.

"My foreign-sounding last name has always been an issue.

The fact that someone can't say your name I think automatically leads people to be kind of shy around you. There's that intangible where you have to schmooze and win people over in order to get ahead, and I've felt it hard to do that networking thing. I do ascribe it to people's discomfort or lack of comfort with folks who don't look like them."

⟜ ⟜

Sometimes insensitivity is not about what is said but about workplace decisions that result in minorities being assigned to controversial projects that are personally offensive.

⟜ ⟜

Sharon Ross* tells a delicious story about how her law firm was oblivious to how its attorneys of color, and their allies, would react to the firm deciding to represent a company that once traded African slaves.

"I worked for a firm that held itself out as a place that promoted diversity and had quite a few programs that on their face would benefit minorities. But then there was an instance where the firm allowed a particular racially charged case, a reparations case, to come in and assigned the case to a minority person and it caused a lot of uproar at the firm. I felt that I was excluded in that we, the associates of color, were never consulted with respect to that type of case. Had I been in the majority, that type of case would have never been brought to the firm. The firm's management said that they had been approached before about representing the Nazis but they chose not to because of what the Nazis did to the Jews, and so on. So they did not have any problems not representing the Nazis.

"But in this case, because it was a client who had been sued for reparations it didn't even occur to the firm that it would have been an issue for the racial minorities who worked for the firm and that the firm should have consulted us and taken our temperature to find out how we felt about it. I felt that because of the minority group I was in, being an associate of color, I was on the outside and I had no influence and I was not contacted with respect to this particular case.

"In fact, the firm's decision to accept this case led to a mass exodus of minority lawyers from the firm as a result. Considering that we didn't have that many black people to begin with, over a period of time six or seven and maybe ten black attorneys left—and there were probably even more than that. That's a lot considering that most firms don't even have that many.

"The firm considered the numbers to be so significant that they brought in diversity consultants and begged the minority lawyers to not take any action until the firm had all these meetings to discuss the issue. It had not occurred to the firm before that black attorneys would leave when the firm accepted a reparations case.

"You would think that it would have occurred to them because there was a minority partner who was in charge of the gate keeping. I guess she was asleep at the wheel at the time. She claimed that she was busy and didn't have a chance to look at the reparations case.

"In essence, I feel that since the firm held itself out as promoting diversity and having all these programs that favor minorities that this should never have happened. The only reason why it happened was because the aggrieved party was a minority. It just was not as significant for the firm to lose a huge client.

"To be honest, I was torn. I had always loved and respected the firm for what it stood for. I had been the beneficiary of a lot of the programs that the firm implemented. So when this happened, I almost thought that maybe what the firm had done in the past was more marketing than anything. It was so easy for me to turn the other way. I was ready to leave myself. But when the firm approached us and was very apologetic about the situation, I felt like you should give people a chance to redeem themselves. I actually encouraged people to at least listen to the dialogue or to have the conversation with the firm to see if there was much they could do because there were a lot of other places that really couldn't give a hoot about what their minority lawyers thought because we are the minority.

"I felt like the firm cared once I saw that they went through the process of getting a diversity consultant and held meetings to get a sense of what approach the firm should follow. So, based on those efforts on the part of the firm, I changed my view."

⟢ ⟣

Sharon's firm probably did not intend to offend its attorneys of color. The firm just failed to consider its attorneys when deciding to represent a new client. Although the firm had a clear sensibility as far as their Jewish attorneys were concerned, it had not communicated enough with African-American attorneys and other attorneys of color. As more and more African-Americans joined the firm, there was definitely a need to gauge the sensibilities of this new and growing population within the firm.

Organizations often do not realize how changes in their employee and client demographics may also require a few tweaks to their social traditions. For instance, some companies pride themselves on sporting events, which tend to be male dominated. However, such events, while open to everyone, still have a tendency to exclude women.

⟢ ⟣

Susannah Burke* is a Caucasian lawyer who practices law in Alabama and has watched her firm hire more women attorneys but fail to welcome them into the fold. As the mother of a little boy, she is sensitive to the time management and business development issues that many of the other women in the firm face. Here, she describes how gender-related events make her and female clients feel excluded. "I think primarily it comes down to marketing for my job. A lot of times the firm will market specifically toward men. I know that they may not necessarily intend to do that but they plan events like a PGA golf tournament. They took a bunch of clients to a PGA golf tournament in Atlanta. That's great, but that's not something I'm interested in doing. I felt like one, I was excluded, and two, that there were female clients who were excluded. The invitation was extended to everyone, but because the subject matter was geared more toward men and all the clients that attended were men it was not something that I felt comfortable attending. I did not attend.

"The firm does host events that are more general. They host cocktail parties and things. But in response to events like the PGA golf tournament, the firm came up with a women's marketing group where we try to target more female clients so we have our female attorneys participating. I just feel like that's the wrong way to go about it. Why does everything have to be geared toward one specific group? Why can't we have more things that are applicable to everybody? I feel like there are ways to market toward women and men. You can do that within the context of one party as opposed to limiting it to one particular group.

"In the context of the large cocktail parties that we have, probably the women are going to migrate toward each other. It tends to happen. There's a way to market within that. At the same time at least you're not saying, 'Oh, well you have to work with me.' You could say, 'There's a guy who works downstairs who does the kind of work you're interested in, client, so I would like to introduce you to him.' As opposed to when we are completely segregated we limit ourselves in terms of marketing. That initial bond could come from woman to woman contact, but at least you still have the men there so that you can introduce everybody and promote the firm as a whole.

"I felt frustrated. I felt like the firm was not considering everyone's feelings. They only considered the people who were planning the event, who incidentally were all men.

"The women's marketing group was created in light of several events like the golf event where men were going out and the women felt excluded. So there was a woman associate, who is now a partner, who decided to start the women's marketing group. We've done events specifically geared toward women. In the fall we do a wine tasting. Only women in the community are invited. Now several of the men in the firm have gotten a little bit frustrated by that because they would like to participate in the wine tasting as well.

"Having the women's group is also frustrating because it is just one more committee meeting that I have to attend and participate in."

⟶ ⟵

Tom Romano* is a Caucasian law firm partner in his 40s who one would not immediately think would relate to Susannah's experience. However, as a religious minority, he has encountered his fair share of insensitivity through his law firm's traditions. "I'll start with the characteristic that's not the most acute, but the one that arguably fits within a protected class—religion. I was raised Catholic. I'm a mutt in terms of my background. I may have even had some Jewish in my background but that's kind of murky. I was raised Catholic. My father's side was predominantly Polish and my mother's side was predominantly Pennsylvania Dutch and Germanic. I stopped practicing Catholicism and considered myself an agnostic.

"When I worked for a predominantly Jewish firm, I felt a little uncomfortable that I was not taking time off for the Jewish holidays. Ironically, I felt uncomfortable when I was working on Rosh Hashanah and Yom Kippur. I felt left out. In the history of things, my firm was one of those firms created for Jews to feel comfortable because they were not let into the white shoe firms.

"I ended up marrying a Jewish woman and we're raising our daughter Jewish and I've even given some thought to converting, but I have not had the time.

"At my current firm, which is historically Irish and Italian and heavily Catholic, I felt a little weird and uncomfortable when I took off for a Jewish holiday. I felt like I had to explain myself. No one did anything that I considered to be discriminatory. Ironically, I have been on both sides of that Jewish versus Christian feeling like you are in the outsider group. No one explicitly made any comments about my religious observances. At my current firm, I do remember when one or two of the other attorneys started to talk about wanting to go home early to prepare meals for the Jewish holidays, our internal counsel asked me for help in understanding the situation better so that they could address the situation properly, which was actually a good thing. Ignorance is part of the problem and it's always a good thing to get more information. They recognized that they were not that used to the situation and they needed to get more used to it.

"The underlying theory is that even if no one is deliberately or consciously doing anything to try to make you feel like an outsider, you can still feel like an outsider. For instance at my firm, they have Friday evening cocktail parties and they never would have done this at my former predominantly Jewish law firm. I try to go home for Shabbat to see my wife and daughter. It's our one guaranteed family night to be together. It's not a big deal if I really need to stay. I've never asked for the firm to change it at this point and don't really see a need to. Ultimately, I would have felt more comfortable if the firm didn't have the cocktail parties on Friday nights."

ADVICE FOR MANAGERS

Offensive comments, insensitive work assignments and hurtful behavior in the workplace are often accompanied by numerous repercussions. According to a 2000 *American Demographics* article, 37% of workers admitted that rude co-workers or clients add to workplace stress. As indicated by the testimonials, insensitive co-workers and managers tested the patience levels of many of the people I interviewed. Insensitivity can definitely become a source of workplace stress. Workplace stress costs employers high turn-over rates and sometimes lawsuits. A 2004 *Customer Inter@ction Solutions* article, "Workplace Stress Sucks $300 Billion Annually from Corporate Profits," brought the stress issue out of the shadows of being a soft cost and raised awareness about its impact on the corporate bottom line.

Bidirectional communication between employee affinity groups and senior management is a useful tool that smart organizations use to test their policies and business decisions. Companies like Darden Restaurants and Macy's have used their affinity groups to avoid culturally offensive marketing campaigns and improve their advertising to minority communities. Affinity groups are ideal for shaping the organization's business policies.

Sharon Ross's firm would have greatly benefited by proposing the reparations case to its affinity groups before deciding to represent such a divisive client. Affinity groups can be more than just party planning committees.

Organizations should not be fooled that because their employees are toughing out racist, sexist, and homophobic jokes, they are not affected by the stress of the situation. Stress can result in burnout, low morale, drug use, and violence. I'm sure that the professionals I interviewed took great pains to exercise restraint from clobbering insensitive people at work.

→≡ ≡←

Insensitivity not only exposes organizations to employment lawsuits and complaints, but it also diminishes worker productivity. For example, Lorna Williams, a young attorney in the telecommunications industry, feels the added stress of constantly working against her manager's close-minded beliefs about her age and gender.

"My supervisors will use certain words like, 'You're just a girl.' I'm thinking to myself, no matter how much you build your credibility, they may still see you like that. It makes me adapt and want to prove that I'm not just a girl. So it's an extra pressure that you really don't need as a minority. There's already so much that you're dealing with, you don't want that too. I was just thinking, after all, I'm still happy with my decision to work for my current employer, but those types of things can make your day go slower because these are the extra things you have to conquer. You get tired."

→≡ ≡←

Insensitivity in the workplace is even more unbearable now that on average, people spend between 8 and 12 hours at work, not because they want to, but because job demands compel them to do so. According to a Fairleigh Dickinson article, "employees work more today than they did 25 years ago—the equivalent of a 13th month every year." Each time a company closes or downsizes a unit, the work of the severed employees does not disappear; it is absorbed by the remaining employees.

Apart from the scenarios raised in the testimonials, how can managers know what will offend a minority employee? Unfortunately, it is impossible to write a book including all of the comments, jokes, emails, and behavior that will offend. However, I can suggest that managers should exercise common sense as a litmus test for whether your words will offend. I once heard a really good rule of thumb for determining offensive conduct: if you would not say something to your grandmother, then you probably should not say it in the workplace.

When organizations take the high road, and rid their work environments of insensitive behavior and stand up for what is right, they make employees into their biggest advocates and cheerleaders.

❧ ❦

Linda Chavez* fondly remembers a time when a senior-level colleague put a cocky client in his place when he made an insensitive remark about her. "I worked on deals outside of the US and I was once traveling with a senior associate and a partner. We went to Spain to work on a transaction. The client was a bank and the conference room we were working in was filled with men. I was the only woman; I was a second-year associate.

"At one point, while working on an information memorandum, one of the clients, a bank executive, made a really inappropriate remark. I can't even remember what it was, but he used my name in a way that was just clearly inappropriate. There are ways in Spanish that you can play with words.

"The senior associate looked him in the eye—now we're in a room with 15 people and we are all drafting—and said, 'Jose, does that really amuse you? Do you think that your wife would be proud of you for saying that? I think we should get back to work and if you could please focus on work and think about the things you say, that would be helpful, and if you could treat Linda with respect that would be helpful.'

"I felt great. I love that associate to this day. It completely embarrassed the bank executive in a room with all his colleagues. So the client, this banker idiot, was clueless while my colleague nipped the situation in the bud and dealt with him directly and publicly.

"The firm made it a practice not to hire only the best and brightest. It made a point to hire people who had outside interests or other careers, e.g., doctors and nurses. So the people tended to be more worldly and have other interests and weren't just third-generation lawyers. Hiring people who were diverse in background might have contributed to the open and inclusive environment I experienced."

⟶⟶ ⟵⟵

ADVICE FOR PROFESSIONALS AND STUDENTS

It is important to realize that people still say and do the most unbelievable things. I like to think that the insensitive comments and behavior on "The Office"—NBC's hit television sit-com—are so over the top that they only make for good entertainment, but every now and then I come across a lawsuit that makes the show's scenarios seem gentle. "The Office" follows the daily interactions of a group of idiosyncratic office employees via a documentary film crew's cameras. The office manager, and lead character, Michael Scott, thinks that he is attuned to the issues of diversity in the workplace, but instead he is clueless and uses outdated stereotypes to inform his interactions with employees of color, LGBT (lesbian, gay, bisexual or transgendered) employees, and women—basically, anyone who is not like him.

There was an episode where Michael outed Oscar, a gay character, and kissed him on the lips to show his acceptance of gay people. After Oscar brought a discrimination complaint against the company, which was quickly settled, he made a very slick and astute assessment about insensitivity in the workplace. When Oscar returned from his "gaycation"—the term Michael coined to describe Oscar's time away from the office while his harassment complaint was being handled—he quickly realized that while the company may have learned its lesson, Michael did not. As Oscar drove into the company parking lot driving the Lexus sports utility vehicle he received from the harassment settlement, Michael kept referring to Oscar as his gay friend. Oscar was not just another employee; he was now the gay guy. While Oscar was bothered because Michael obviously did not get it, Oscar had second thoughts about the value of changing Michael's behavior. Instead, he thought, let Michael make his stupid comments about gay people. Eventually Michael's outrageous comments and behavior would give Oscar enough evidence to bring another claim. Oscar had his eye on a home theater.

Remember, insensitivity sometimes evolves into actionable discrimination in the workplace and there are now remedies to curb outrageous conduct. Laws such as Title VII of the 1964 Civil Rights Act and similar state and city statutes prohibit disparate treatment based on a protected class. (Protected classes include race, color, gender, national origin, and religion.) Keep a journal of anything uncomfortable that has occurred. Your contemporaneous notes will keep your memories fresh and enable you to substantiate your story for your supervisor or human resources.

Depending on the situation, try to find a direct and tactful way to let the individuals know that you do not find their humor funny or that their conduct has offended you. The traditional advice is to "act nice" so that offenders will see the error of their ways. When someone hurts you, you don't have to play nice, you have to play smart. Have a trusted cadre of friends and advisors whom you can easily contact when insensitivity in the workplace strikes. Often, we may find something offensive yet objectively it is harmless. These advisors can help you to put a situation into perspective and devise a strategy for handling it. You should have at least one advisor on your speed dial.

Also, try to have influential allies in your office who can address a situation with an offending manager on a peer level. A complaint coming from an intern or a junior-level employee sounds much different, and is accordingly treated differently, than a complaint coming from a senior-level manager.

Also, keep in mind that people are capable of changing. When I shared my book with some of my colleagues, they were surprised that I wrote a book from the perspective that there are people who care about improving diversity and advancing equality in the workplace. I really do believe that there are enough people in the majority who really care about improving workplace relationships, especially with those who are in the minority.

⇀⇒   ⇐↼

For example, Cassandra Phillips* told me about an instance in her career that exhibits the power of awareness and the change that is possible in all of us. "I did experience a situation where being a woman made me a bit of an outsider in terms of being accepted at a private club. I was in Paris, and I was newly appointed as the American representative for the International Chamber of Commerce Court of Arbitration. I was meeting with the arbitration committee. It was the first time I was meeting them. I was very excited to be coming from New York and meeting with these lawyers who were arbitration experts.

"I went to the designated location at the appointed hour and when I walked into the club, the person greeting me, a man, said in French that I was not allowed or permitted to enter the club through the main steps. For a moment, my first thought was I must not understand his French so I had him repeat himself. It was clear I understood him. And then I thought, is this because I'm black or because I'm a woman? Just as I was thinking that, an older white woman approached and he would not allow her to enter the club either through the main steps. And I felt a bit relieved that it wasn't because I was black; it was clear it was because I was a woman.

"After some negotiations and explanation, it turned out that this club did not allow women to use the main stairway to go up to the private dining rooms because there were nude portraits. I don't mean pornographic, but just paintings and the club thought they would be offensive to women. So they did not want women to use the main stairwell. When I explained that I was expected for a business luncheon and there had to be some other solution, they took me around the back entrance of the club and up the side steps. So I entered the room through the kitchen and side entrance.

"There was a moment where I debated whether I should go through the back stairs or not but then I wanted to prove a point by coming in through the back way.

"All the men in the meeting (because there weren't any women on the committee) were mortified by what happened. It never dawned on them that this would happen. After the lunch, they thanked me for attending the meeting. At the end of the lunch, the men went in solidarity down the back stairs with me and never had lunch again at that place.

"I felt like it was a life lesson for all of us. I could have easily decided to not attend. But I decided, I'm here to do a job and I'm going to do the job and prove the point by showing them what I had to go through to get to the meeting. It was not something they intended. It was just something they never thought about because they never had a woman in the position before. I thought that their reaction, their apologizing, going forward with the meeting and walking down the back stairs with me, said a lot about how they wanted to rectify the mistake. I went on to stay in that position for a number of years."

CHAPTER 5

INABILITY TO RECOVER
FROM MISTAKES

As hard as we may try, we often fall short of the glory of being perfect. In line with the theme, "Failure is not in the falling down but how you get up," how we recover is greatly affected and determined by those who are on the receiving end of our mistakes. People in the minority are often led to believe by our parents and mentors that we have to be twice as good as our majority counterparts, in part, because people are less forgiving of our mistakes and expect us to fail.

These theories about double standards partly grow out of the observation that people in the majority are often forgiven much sooner than people in the minority. Let's use Mark Rich as an example. This billionaire financier was indicted for evading more than $48 million in taxes and charged with running illegal oil deals. He received a pardon from President Bill Clinton and today lives comfortably in Switzerland.

Even in the court of public opinion, offensive white radio personalities are quickly forgiven for their antics by other white men. During the 2007 Don Imus fiasco where he called members of the Rutgers women's basketball team "nappy-headed hos," Republican and Democratic presidential candidates, respectively, Senators John McCain and Christopher Dodd condemned his actions but then quickly issued their forgiveness and even agreed to make future appearances on his show, which fortunately was cancelled.

Yet, minorities, African-Americans in particular, have a much harder time making a comeback. How many of you remember—or even know of—Janet Cooke? Ms. Cooke was a *Washington Post* journalist who won a Pulitzer Prize for a story about an 8-year-old heroin addict, and she was later exposed as a fraud for concocting the story. Her punishment started with rightfully stripping her of the award, but the public and the journalism community never forgave her. She disappeared from journalism and public life, and was never able to recover from her mistake. During an interview with NBC almost 10 years after the incident, Ms. Cooke was clearly unforgiven for her mistake. Ms. Cooke was working as a salesperson in a retail clothing store and the interviewer commented that her inability to ever work in journalism and her permanent fall from public life were what she deserved for lying.

While Ms. Cooke's offense was clearly egregious, are all public figures that are caught lying eternally punished for their misdeeds? In July 2007, President Bush answered the question by commuting the sentence of I. Lewis "Scooter" Libby when a jury convicted him of perjury and sentenced him to 2½ years in prison. President Bush rushed to the aid of his fallen friend and colleague, who happened to also be white and male. Mr. Libby also had the support of Fred Thompson, a Hollywood actor and potential presidential candidate who led his defense fund and called for the pardon. Mr. Thompson was quoted by Washingtonpost.com as saying, "This will allow a good American who has done a lot for his country to resume his life."

While some may argue that the Libby situation and Ms. Cooke's are vastly different—one was a political favor while the other dealt with ethics in journalism—the bottom line is that both individuals lied. Libby's offense was probably even more dangerous than Ms. Cooke's because he lied to FBI agents and obstructed a federal investigation into whether administration officials illegally disclosed the name of a CIA officer. Ms. Cooke's concocted story about an eight-year-old heroin addict may have caused *Washington Post* readers to question the veracity of the news. But Mr. Libby's offense compromised the American justice system and could have caused great physical harm to the CIA officer whose identity was leaked.

The Reverend Al Sharpton is another example of America's good memory when it comes to what they perceive as mistakes minorities make. Rev. Sharpton's credibility is still questioned 20 years after supporting Tawana Brawley, a black teenager who accused white law enforcement officers of sexual assault, which many thought was a hoax. MSNBC's David Gregory did not hesitate to remind viewers of Rev. Sharpton's involvement with the "scandal" during Don Imus's controversy.

As people in the minority, we watch how the double standard of performance and forgiveness plays out and we do not expect anything different in the workplace. When our colleagues in the majority make mistakes, they are forgiven and put on the path to redemption. We see how our colleagues in the majority sometimes get extra coaching and attention from managers and consultants to brush up on their skills. Yet when we make similar mistakes, if we do not have someone from the majority invested in our success, it is almost impossible to ever make a comeback.

Although we all make mistakes, how we're dealt with makes all the difference. Are you given a second chance or are you forever marked as the underskilled employee?

⟶⟫ ⟨⟵

Tanesha Robinson* understands what it is like to not have an opportunity to come back from a mistake. Tanesha is a Haitian woman who accomplished an almost impossible feat by graduating from a second-tier law school and becoming an associate at a first-tier corporate law firm in New York City. Although she worked tirelessly to churn out quality work, she found that people were more willing to work around her as opposed to with her.

"I had instances where I submitted an assignment and I was told that what I handed in was not specifically what was asked for. My work was not to someone's liking. Instead of the person giving me back the assignment and outlining what was wrong or right, explaining what should have been done and what was required, I was basically told, 'I'll do it myself or I'll have someone else do it,' rather than showing me how to do it right the first or second time around. Whereas, my Caucasian counterparts and classmates were basically sat down and mentored and reviewed the assignment line by line as to how it should be done the next time and they were given second opportunities to do additional work where I was not.

"Usually these encounters were with senior associates but in one instance this occurred with a partner. I had given her an assignment she requested. She never got back to me. I asked her numerous times if she had any comments on the document that I produced. If there were any comments, please let me know. I never heard from her. I decided to check the status of the document in the firm's shared folder on the computer system and I saw that the document was totally redone by someone else and I was never told why my work was wrong or how it should have been done differently. So apparently that partner didn't feel that she should have come and spoken to me about how she wanted the assignment. She either did it herself or had someone else do it and never got back to me or told me, 'this is the proper way to do it.' So I never had the opportunity to learn from my mistake.

"This experience made me feel pretty inferior. It made me feel as though my contribution to the firm was not appreciated or valued and that the work environment is not nurturing and mentoring to a minority like myself. So I really felt like I was not given the opportunity that my Caucasian counterparts have to really learn and hone and shape the skills that I need as an attorney."

⊷⊶

Tanesha was cheated of the opportunity to correct her substantive work mistakes. Her managers and superiors did not inform her of her mistakes earlier in her career at the firm and instead tricked her into thinking that she was doing well. One by one, partners and senior associates did not want to work with her. Eventually, Tanesha, who was once deemed valuable by the firm, was branded as incompetent after six years and was asked to leave her firm. Fortunately, another firm saw Tanesha's talents and scooped her up immediately. She is now in a more nurturing environment where her managers value her contributions and do not overlook what she has to offer the firm.

⊷⊶

Sometimes the hardest mistakes to recover from involve what we said or did in a tense situation. How many times do you wish that you had a time machine to go back in time to retract a comment? Most of us have been in situations where we wished that we reacted differently. People in the minority sometimes find that their faux pas are not so quickly forgotten or forgiven.

⊷⊶

Wade Tong* is a young television reporter of color who

learned a lesson in double standards when he tried to advocate for himself. "One particular ratings period, my boss said, 'Hey, I want you to do the morning show.' That would have required me coming into the studio, doing the morning show and then anchoring my show at 11:30 and then leave at noon. Well, I did it on and off to fill in during the ratings period but I didn't like it. That's not what I was hired to do. I was hired to work 9-5, Monday through Saturday. I like to anchor my show and then go out and find stories for the afternoon show. I filled in several times and I never complained. That's my policy. No matter what happens, I just go in. I've never called in sick; I never miss a day of work. I'm always there at my time slot. If I'm supposed to be there at 9 am, I'm there by 8:30 am every day.

"Then one day on the set, one of my co-anchors asked me, 'Hey, are you going to be the permanent morning show reporter?' I said I hope not. That's not what I came here to do. I was bothered by this arrangement, so I went to my news director and maybe I handled it the wrong way but I said, 'I didn't really come here to be a morning show reporter. I came here to anchor the mid-day news. I was in Cincinnati. If I wanted to do a morning show I would have gone to Atlanta or Chicago to be a reporter. I'm a little concerned.' The news director said, 'You know, I have a plan for the morning show but I'm not going to tell anybody what it is yet. I told you that I just need you to do the morning show temporarily.' I finished out my time on the morning show.

"When it was time to renegotiate my contract, during my review, my news director brought the situation back up. He said, 'One thing that really bothered me is that you came to me with this 'big anchor' ego, like 'I didn't leave Cincinnati to do your little morning show.'

"Now that is not what I said at all. In fact, I just said that I was concerned. My news director said, 'Well, to me it was like you were too good for our morning show.' I told him that I disagreed with him because from the day I was hired, anytime the station called me, I would even jump out of bed in the middle of the night and go cover stories about fires, shootings, or whatever. The news director said, 'Well you came across as though you were this big time anchor and you were too good for our morning show. This really bothered me.' He said, 'I'm not going to renew your contract. We're just going to go month to month because I just don't feel like you want to be here and I don't want anybody here who doesn't want to be here.' That really, really upset me. I thought about it and thought maybe I should take responsibility for it. Maybe I brought this on myself. Maybe I didn't handle things the right way because I try not to complain.

"The news director eventually hired someone for the morning show to be a flat-out morning show reporter. However, while he was looking for a morning show person, he changed my co-anchors. He tried out at least three women at the anchor desk. He put an Asian woman with me at the anchor desk and I thought that she did very well. I thought she had energy, personality, we got along well. In fact, we're friends so it's easy. I thought she did a good job. He brought in this person who is his favorite, a white girl, and said, 'I have an opportunity for you. You can do the morning show and then anchor the 11:30 news.' She said, 'I don't know if I want to do that because I don't want to be a morning show reporter.' He said, 'But you have this great opportunity to anchor the 11:30 news.' Her response was, 'I'm concerned because when I leave here I want to leave here as a reporter/anchor. If I do the morning show I would be limiting myself to doing live shots.' He got mad at her and said, 'Don't expect any favors from me.' When I heard about this I thought maybe he is fair. The news director was upset with her and opened up the offer to do the morning show to everyone else.

"He eventually gave the anchor position to that white woman. I just assumed that she apologized to the news director and asked for another chance. But, she and I were in the make-up room getting ready and she goes, 'When the news director first came to me, he said that he had a great opportunity for me and I told him that I didn't want to do it. And then the news director said, 'Well, I don't want to have two reporters anchoring a show and then trying to turn stories on short deadlines.' She said that she initially turned the morning show down and then after two weeks of having the Asian woman anchor, the news director called her into his office and said, 'Do it for me. Just try it. If you don't like it then don't do it.' I thought, that's funny, when it was me, he told me that I had this huge anchor ego.'"

⇢⇒ ⇐⇠

The double standard in forgiveness is most apparent in the disciplinary scheme. There are times when a supervisor will give one employee some slack when he messes up. He may bend the rules for an employee who shows up to work late because the employee is usually punctual or is a top performer. A boss may decide to overlook an employee's workplace infractions because they have developed a personal relationship and a boss does not want to come down hard on his friend.

The ability to overlook one employee's infractions over another's, though, has the detrimental effect of marginalizing one employee. While an employer may be instilling good employer-employee relations with one employee, he is potentially ostracizing the employee he chooses to penalize. Often when employees in the minority notice that they are the employee who is treated by the book while their majority counterparts are not, this creates an environment that says that discriminatory discipline is ok, and that discrimination, in general, is an acceptable practice.

❧ ❧

Raheem Mohammad,* a television executive in his 30s, remembers when he was reprimanded more harshly than his white woman counterpart for the same exact offense. "There was an incident where I was severely reprimanded by my direct report for what he called a dereliction of duty when we were at a regional convention in Newport, Rhode Island, and I took this person I was dating at the time with me. She ended up being around for the first day of the convention. My supervisor wrote me up and said that I was being detrimental to the company; that I was representing the cable network, and this is something that he didn't ever want to see again. He came within two sentences of saying, 'I'm going to have to let you go.' I took that very seriously. For me, it was extremely hurtful because I didn't think that I did anything that was detrimental to my work. However, in the evening I did take time to be with my girlfriend. And that's really where his point was. According to my supervisor, I was on call 24 hours a day.

"So, as it turns out, a couple of years later when I didn't work in that territory anymore, a young lady who was Caucasian ended up going to one of the events at the same convention with her then ex-husband. She did not want to go alone. The interesting thing that happened to her was that she got the same speech from the same supervisor that I received but she was not put on notice that she had 90 days to clean up her act.

"That was the only time in my work history that I felt that there could be discriminatory proceedings because why is it that I'm almost fired? Although I did not share the details of my reprimand, she shared her story with me. I asked her what was the outcome and she said that the supervisor really laid into her and that she felt really bad. But what didn't happen was that she was not written up, and her position was not threatened. She was read the riot act and then everything was ok. I didn't quite understand the difference if it was the same dereliction of duties. Why didn't she receive the same level of admonishment from the senior person? That was the only time in my 18 years that I was treated differently because I am a minority. The supervisor and my woman co-worker were both Caucasian and I was not. As it turns out, I left within three months after that whole incident."

⇢ ⇠

ADVICE FOR MANAGERS

We all make mistakes and should acknowledge that no one is perfect. However, in our pursuit to impress clients and increase revenue, we are sometimes excessively harsh when employees make mistakes. Punishing an employee, eternally, for a small mistake is counterproductive to workplace harmony and performance.

⇢ ⇠

For example, Kendra Washington* was one of those senior law firm associates who threw junior associates out with the bathwater. She was busy trying to impress the law firm's partners and couldn't care less about any junior associate's professional development. After wasting the diamonds in the rough who surrounded her, she realized that she was wasting valuable resources and talent all because she would not take a moment to coach someone.

"I'm about to reveal a major secret about attorneys—well, it's only a secret to those who have never worked in a law firm.

Attorneys are some of the worst people-managers. For all our intelligence, and access to leadership training (some of us even hold M.B.A.'s in management), some of us still do not know how to effectively manage others, especially when it comes to giving feedback. I could never understand how some of the brightest legal minds did not provide constructive criticism and valuable guidance to their associates and staff. Instead, partners would send clandestine emails to other partners about an associate, or just flat out complain to anyone who would listen—even the clients. This was an inexplicable phenomenon to me until I managed my first summer associate.

"I asked the summer associate to find a statute I needed for a writing assignment. That was the first and last substantive assignment I gave to her. I didn't give her too many details about the project because I assumed that what I needed was simple and self-explanatory. It was simple and self-explanatory to me because, of course, I understood what I needed. Circular reasoning is never a good thing, especially when giving assignments.

"The summer associate was going into her third year of law school and had worked for the firm for two summers in a row. She was from a wealthy area of Connecticut and seemed smart enough to research a statute.

"The next day she proudly walked into my office with a sheet of yellow paper torn off of a legal pad. She had written, or actually scrawled, the statute in red ink. I was speechless. I was so stunned that I could barely find the words to utter a polite 'thank you.' I didn't think that I would have to tell a law student (1) to type the information I needed, and (2) if it had to be written, not to use red ink!

"A few days later, she asked me for feedback and I had tons, but I could not express my thoughts. I was actually offended by her submission. I didn't even read it. I tucked it away in my desk drawer, researched the issue myself, and went on with my day. In the days that followed, she would stop by my office asking for feedback. She desperately wanted to know if she did a good job and if I had the information I needed.

"I suffered from the same problem that ails most managers. Often, we will not provide feedback unless we really care about a person's professional development. Honestly, I was so swamped with work that I didn't want to invest the time in the summer associate. I thought, if I have to tell this woman not to use red ink when completing assignments, she is too much work for me and I don't have the time.

"In hindsight, I wish that I had managed the summer associate differently. I should have given her the opportunity to redeem herself. While my experiences (and common sense) taught me that red pen and handwritten briefs are unacceptable, I should have given the summer associate the opportunity to explain herself. Was the office out of black or blue pens? Did she not have access to a computer or word processor? Was she under a time crunch? This may have been the first time that anyone told her that red ink is not acceptable in the workplace. Now, if she made the same mistake again, then I would have been justified to move on, but without investing five minutes of feedback in this associate, I cost myself time and wasted a potentially valuable resource."

◦➠ ◦➠◦

Kendra finally realized that if a candidate was good enough for the firm to hire, more likely than not the employee should be good enough to develop.

Underperforming employees often do not know exactly what the problem was with their work because managers do not take the time to explain the shortcomings. Managers should try to be as specific as possible when describing where the employee went wrong. If the employee turned in a writing assignment that was not to your standards, explain where the employee should try to improve. Was it a grammatical issue? Content? Organization? If so, zero in on the issue so that the employee has a clearer idea of what he or she should address.

Managers should try to create ways to develop their employees' skills and abilities. A manager may try to assign a point person to work closely with the employee who is perceived as underperforming. That person would be easily accessible to the employee to answer any questions or provide feedback on projects.

For years, organizations have quietly given underperforming white men and women coaching on everything from sales techniques to speech therapy.

For instance, I know this law firm partner who invested heavily in a perky white woman who, as she described, "Didn't know shit," when she was first hired. The partner invited the associate to her country home on the weekends, invited her to practice oral arguments in front of her husband—who was one of the best prosecutors in New York City—and continues to give her endless encouragement. Today that associate is just as good as any of the other associates in the firm.

Coaching is an option that should also be made available to employees in the minority. As stated earlier, minority employees will invest their best in an organization that invests in them.

Not giving an employee in the minority the opportunity to redeem himself can become an expensive practice for the organization. When a manager comes down hard on persons in the minority in the workplace for making a mistake while making allowances for other employees, employees in the minority start to question whether they are working for the right organization. These employees may feel less valuable to the organization and as a result decide to leave. Patience is not only a virtue but also a cost-saver.

Honesty and fairness, theoretically, are two of the most simple—but realistically most difficult to implement—characteristics to guide managers through decision-making. When managers make choices based on what is right, they make it more difficult for employees to make accusations of unfairness. Employees sometimes know when they are required to jump through extra hoops to get the same treatment their colleagues in the majority get; people talk. When employees in the minority notice that they are penalized more harshly than their majority counterparts for similar conduct, it ruins office morale and, if egregious enough, may lead to a lawsuit for disparate treatment.

When disciplining employees, ask yourself, are you following company policy for one employee and not the other? Does the punishment for a person in the minority exceed your usual office protocol, even though you are following the written company policy? Are you scrutinizing one employee instead of another because of your personal preferences? If the answers to these questions are "yes," then you may potentially open your organization up to lawsuits.

When people feel as though they have been treated unfairly, they look for justice. Under federal and most state anti-discrimination statutes, employers are prohibited from subjecting an employee to disparate rights and privileges based on protected characteristics—race, age, disability, gender, religion, color, and gender.

Employers are sometimes successful in defending discrimination claims where employees were not similarly treated. However, the company wasted thousands (sometimes millions) of dollars defending an action that carried the stench of discrimination. Is office favoritism worth a trip to the Equal Employment Opportunity Commission?

ADVICE FOR PROFESSIONALS AND STUDENTS

We all appreciate a job well done even when it comes to the most basic things. Many of us have a favorite restaurant, a favorite coffee shop, or a favorite clothing store. The reason why we frequent these establishments and recommend them to our friends is because someone did a good job. The cook did a good job of choosing the food ingredients and preparing them. The coffee shop may have a friendly cashier who works hard to reduce the customers' wait time. The clothing store had skilled seamstresses and designers. You go to these establishments because the cook, cashier and designer do their jobs to your satisfaction. When you complete projects to your boss's and the client's satisfaction, you too will become the go-to person in your office. Try to approach each assignment as the recipient and end-user. Think, how could I complete this assignment so that my boss does not have to do much more to it? Think, what answers can I provide to my boss to assist with this project?

If it has not happened already, there will come a day that you will make a mistake at work and may even be reprimanded. Some employers understand that for any number of reasons your work will not always be perfect. This may have been your first assignment and you did not completely understand the assignment. Or, you may have had an off-day and missed an important deadline. The reality is that you may even make the same mistake twice depending on the difficulty of the project, but you can avoid becoming a repeat offender. While you should strive to be the best at whatever you do, you also want to have a plan for recovering, quickly, from a mishap.

Try to admit and understand the mistake, make a note of it (if necessary), and move on. Dwelling on mistakes does nothing but create unnecessary stress. Our society is built on the backs of survivors who did not allow their mistakes to hamper their success and moved on. (Just think of Martha Stewart after Imclone, Janet Jackson after the Superbowl wardrobe malfunction, or Sean "P. Diddy" Combs after the New Year's Eve shootout where he was charged with illegal weapons possession.)

Be sure to own up to mistakes without over-apologizing. Most managers do not have the patience to hear someone continually saying "I'm sorry." It gets annoying and makes you look wimpy. Most managers just want to know that the employee understands what he or she did wrong and intends to remedy the situation.

Always seek feedback on assignments and don't be afraid to ask for help. There are studies showing that racial minorities are less likely to ask for help than their majority counterparts. How can you compete with your majority counterparts if you're not using the same tools and resources to win the game? When you know what was done right or wrong you can make adjustments and create a model for moving forward. When you do ask questions, try not to ask basic questions that merely gloss over the issues. Instead, ask the specific questions that will guide your work the next time you have a similar assignment. For example, if you have questions about your first meeting with a client and are unsure about what to ask, I would suggest asking your supervisor questions that are more specific than, "What do I do?" Consider asking your supervisor questions like, "What type of information would you suggest I gather from my meeting with the client?" and, "What techniques have you used to gather this information in the past?" Open-ended questions that are focused on what you want to accomplish will yield answers that get you closer to what you are trying to achieve.

Lastly, remember to have faith and confidence in your abilities. We all make mistakes and it is important to remember that everyone has had a setback or two. Do you recall President Bill Clinton's nomination speech at the 1988 Democratic convention? I'm sure he hopes that you don't. His speech was long winded, tedious, and boring. In Washington D.C.'s political circles, that speech—when people remember it—is known as the worst speech ever given at a presidential convention. Did President Clinton disappear after this setback? Of course not. President Clinton learned from that experience and has perfected his speaking abilities to the point where he is now known as one of the best communicators in the world and he earns $250,000 per speech.

CHAPTER 6

AGGRESSIVE COMMUNICATION

At the risk of stating the obvious, no one likes to be yelled at and humiliated in the workplace. In 2006, two Wharton M.B.A. students conducted a study about respect and its relationship to burnout in the workplace. The researchers gathered that "Respect is a way in which employees get entrenched into the workplace and feel that what they do is meaningful."

Aggressive behavior is just one of the many ways an employer can disrespect an employee. Yellers, throwers and other bad actors are nothing but bullies. Bullying is definitely on the rise and is gaining recognition as a national, and international, problem. A quick web search about bullying yielded websites like mytoxicboss.com, bullyingonline.org, and bully-busters.org. There are even institutes that specialize in helping employees to deal with bullies. A *New York Times* article, "Fear in the Workplace: The Bullying Boss," helped confirm the existence of this epidemic. According to the article, some people bully for the "sheer pleasure of exercising power," while others do it to "swat down a threatening subordinate."

⚬

Indiya Harris* dealt with passive-aggressive bullies every-day when she practiced law for a mid-sized firm in New York City. While her superiors rarely raised their voices, their nitpick-ing and needling of her work was their way of asserting control. Indiya recalls an incident in her firm that made her question how much longer she was going to be a bullying partner's victim. "This one instance that I can think of clearly, I was working on a case and the partner and I went to the client's place of business to interview an employee. This employee was adverse to our client. During the course of the interview, I could see that my partner did not like my being there as a black person and as a woman. During the course of the interview, he had me there and I was asking questions, but when he wanted to go off the record he would ask me to step out of the room. We were a team and we were supposed to work together. This partner didn't trust me. It was an age discrimination case and I felt that he assumed that because I was a woman, black and member of a minority group, I would sympathize with the plaintiff more than I would sympathize with our client. From the beginning, that was my feeling. The plaintiff was a white man. We were doing an inves-tigation and I felt that the investigation should be a thorough investigation. The investigation he was doing was a whitewash.

"Our client wanted the investigation to come out one way and the partner was doing everything in his power to see that it came out that way. Instead of doing a regular investigation where you look at all the facts and then you make a determination at the end, the partner had his conclusion and he was trying to put the facts to the conclusion. So, every time there would be a question or an instance that our client may be liable or may be a wrong-doer, he would ask me to step out of the room. I just did as he asked because I felt that one, he was going to take me off the case, which he did eventually, and two, I couldn't question him in front of the client and if I asked him to step out of the room with me, he wouldn't have done it so there was nothing for me to do.

"I felt frustrated and angry. This did not affect my work product, but it did affect the partner's work product because he became super critical of me. Things got out of control when he didn't even trust me to write up the investigation notes. For instance, I interviewed an employee who used the word 'seconded,' which he defined as he was working for a law firm and the law firm loaned him out to our client—who was at that time a client of that law firm. I took for granted that the definition was right because it sounded right. We were asking him pro forma questions, you know, nothing substantive. You know, warm-up questions that you would ask like, 'when did you start at the firm, when did you finish.' So this guy's answer was, 'Before I was hired as a full-time employee, I was *seconded* from the years blah blah blah.' And we asked him what was seconded, what did that mean? I was in charge of writing up the notes, and I put in the word seconded and explained his definition as a footnote. I did it for two reasons: one, when I went on the internet and looked up the definition it seemed similar and the word usage seemed consistent, and two, it wasn't a big deal. Well, when the partner got it he sent me an email asking me if I looked it up in Webster's dictionary and why didn't I put the definition in the notes. It was clearly his way of bullying. And that's the word, bullying me, trying to get me to take myself off the case. It was a hostile work environment. I define it as a hostile work environment. It was extremely hostile for blacks and women and anyone who was different. I felt like an outsider because I was the only African-American female with children in the firm. You were looked upon as untrustworthy. That is the word, untrustworthy. They can not trust your writing, they can not trust your analysis, they can not trust your not sympathizing with the other side. They don't trust you or want you to be there."

⟶⟢ ⟣⟵

Not too long after that incident, Indiya decided that she was too smart and too good of an attorney to work in an environment where she was bullied. After hoarding away enough of her $200,000-a-year salary, she left the firm to open up her own firm.

PHYSICAL AGGRESSION

While I have never been threatened with a hurling stapler or any other office supply, I have seen and heard of all types of abuse in the workplace. In 15 years of working—from a high school job at a local hospital to working in law firms—I have overheard vicious arguments where people used more expletives than nouns. Yet, I have never seen anything productive accomplished by physical and verbal aggression.

⟶⟢ ⟣⟵

LaTanya Smith* became the victim of old-fashioned bullying early in life. She was a college freshman and quickly learned that not all adults act like grown-ups. "My mother hated my first job when I was in college. It was a part-time job with my college's campus dining services. 'Dining services!' she would exclaim. 'I didn't send you to school to wash dishes, clean other people's floors or cook other students' food.' Actually, I worked in the administrative office and helped students with their meal card dilemmas. Although I never washed a dish or stepped foot in the cafeteria's kitchen, all my mother could envision was me cleaning trays. Similar to most ambitious West Indian parents, she was a proud woman who wanted nothing but the best for me. She was concerned about the caliber of people I would work for in 'the kitchen.' After my first, and only year on the job, I would agree that she had good reason to be concerned.

"Campus dining definitely was not the type of job with an extensive career track. Most of the student workers did a nine-month stint during the academic year and moved on. There was no succession planning or training for new employees. For the first six months, I was left on my own to figure out the office's procedures and processes. My boss was a lazy woman who mostly used me to get her coffee (with 16 packets of sugar) and cookies from the dining hall rather than helping her with necessary filing, typing and other clerical work. She had stacks of untouched papers on her desk; she was a mess.

"At the end of each month, the office filed its accounts receivable statement with the main office. Well, one month my supervisor could not find the statement. When I walked into the office, my supervisor's boss—who outweighed me by 100 pounds—pulled me by the collar demanding, 'Where is the statement!' She had a menacing smile on her face and thought she was being funny. In her twisted mind, she probably thought she was just joking around. I was not laughing. I was scared. I couldn't believe that this woman, an older woman who signed my paycheck, thought she had license to physically grab me. (If I knew then what I know now, I would have reported her to the dean and the president's office. Based on that stunt, I'm sure that the university would have given me a complimentary life-time meal plan to keep the incident quiet.)

"Instead, I took a less political route. I spoke to the next senior person in the office, my supervisor's boss's boss, who realized that I was upset by the incident and apologized. In the middle of my sheepish and inarticulate retelling of the events, I let it be known that I would not stand for abuse. I didn't know what would happen if I complained but I knew I had to. I could not continue to work for campus dining and keep in my feelings of disgust and humiliation about the situation.

"When I told my mother about the incident, she thought I overreacted. She thought that my boss was being playful by pulling me by the collar like the 'tough guys' do in the movies. My mother and I just didn't see eye to eye. Even though my mom was no big fan of the job, there were benefits that she couldn't deny. I had flexible hours, a complimentary meal plan, and lived within walking distance. She feared that I would lose my job. Fortunately, my boss's boss was understanding and agreed with my assessment of the situation. While no immediate action was taken, I like to think that my complaint had something to do with my lazy supervisor getting fired by the end of the academic school year. And by the way, she later found the missing document on her desk, trapped underneath a pile of other documents I'm sure she thought an office intern lost."

❦ ❦

LaTanya's experience with her physically threatening boss was unsettling but even more curious was her mother's reaction. Given that LaTanya's mother never even wanted her to work for campus dining I was surprised that her mother did not support her decision to report the situation. In search of an explanation that would help make sense of LaTanya's mother's perception of the collar incident, I recalled a conversation with Bruce Tulgan.

Bruce Tulgan is an expert on generational differences and the author of *Managing Generation X*, among many other books. During our conversation he explained the stark differences between how Boomers and my generation react to aggressive behavior from our bosses. "Generation X has a much different point of view about their employment relationships. The older generations were told keep your mouth shut, do what you're told, wait for your boss to notice you, and wait for the long-term rewards to vest. With Gen. X and Y it's today, tomorrow, next week. Any kind of abusive behavior—forget discrimination on the basis of an impermissible classification or reason—is not tolerated. If you don't like the way I dress, too bad. Bye! You throw a stapler at me when you're frustrated? There are all kinds of things that people used to tolerate that Gen. X and Y won't tolerate because relationships in the workplace are more short-term and transactional. The younger and least experienced people start out assuming short-term and transactional, so they'll just go work somewhere else. That's another factor beyond just the expectation. You could be shocked that you are being discriminated against and then say this is going to be a drag if I'm going to be here a long time."

⇢⇥ ⇤⇠

VERBAL AGGRESSION

⇢⇥ ⇤⇠

Shirley Pelosi* was in her 20s when she determined that if she did not confront the office yeller, each day at work would have been a drag. For seven years, Shirley was Director of Marketing and Business Development for an architecture firm in New York City. The firm was 66 years old. It had been started by the father of one of the partners. So there were seven equity partners, and they ranged in age from 40s to 75. They were all men and they were all white. When she had to attend partnership meetings with the partners, it was she and seven guys.

From the moment Shirley started working for the firm she was ambitious. The firm's partners wanted her to do a marketing plan and a marketing budget, which she had never done before. Shirley figured out the ropes on her own. However, her efforts were often overlooked. "I never really let myself get too intimidated by it, but there were moments. The partners would gang up on me and say, 'You don't get it. You're not an architect.' Although I was the only non–licensed professional in the room, I didn't let it get to me. During meetings when they would ask, 'Why are you doing this? Why, why, why?' I had to really know my stuff and stick to my guns. I couldn't let it get in the way of doing my job. It was a triumph. They started to respect my recommendations regarding which projects to accept and reject.

"One of the partners was a yeller and his idea of communicating was yelling. The yeller would walk into my office, shout at me and then walk back to his office. It scared the hell out of me getting yelled at by a guy my dad's age. I told him, if you want me to work here you can not yell at me. You can not treat me like a child. That won his respect.

"Eventually, I left the firm due to a lot of infighting between the partners."

❧

ADVICE FOR MANAGERS

While managers are in a powerful position and can, technically, vent their frustrations on employees by keeping leather whips in the office to scare employees or slamming telephones to the point they shatter—there are bosses who actually engage in this type of behavior—such employers will not win any loyalty contests with their employees, especially minority employees from Generations X and Y. We are the generations that were coddled, not paddled.

Managers should consider the long-range effects of their emotional outbursts and think twice about how they talk to people. Are you raising your voice? Are you speaking to your employee the way in which you would want someone to speak to your daughter or son? Is your aggressive behavior really going to accomplish anything?

Not only does aggressive behavior in the workplace have the potential to reduce your employees' productivity, it sometimes comes with an expensive price tag. In 2006, the National Education Association paid $750,000 to settle a sex discrimination lawsuit that was based on one tyrannical employee's bad behavior. A high-level male supervisor subjected his female employees to yelling, screaming, and profanity-laced verbal attacks. The EEOC's press release described the supervisor as "turning bright red with bulging neck veins as he screamed, coming so close [to the women that] they often felt his saliva spit on their faces." According to the EEOC press release, although the supervisor's harassment was not sexual, the court of appeals did not dismiss the case on the grounds that "harassing conduct does not have to be motivated by lust or blatant misogyny to be illegal sex discrimination."

As you can see, there are serious consequences for hostile behavior in the workplace.

ADVICE FOR PROFESSIONALS AND STUDENTS

Most bullies, essentially, feel inadequate and their hostile behavior is a way of dragging someone else down to their miserable level. Although there are no federal laws against bullying, a workplace may have a policy to address hostile, harassing, or threatening behavior. As with any other issue in the workplace, check with your employee handbook. Depending on the situation, you may also want to report any bullying that rises to threatening behavior to the human resources department.

Going to work, sometimes, requires the same strategies you used on the playground in elementary school. Remember when the playground bully was tamed? It was because someone stood up to him or her. The same concept works with bully bosses. Respectfully, let them know that it is not all right to yell at you. Let the bully know that there is no reason to yell at you. Once you shock a bully by responding and checking his or her behavior, the bully may think twice before doing it again.

⟜ ⟜

Standing up to your boss, however, especially if he is a bully, is not a light matter. There are reasonable and rational concerns that you will be retaliated against or even fired. Natasha Cormen* was a new attorney when she was blindsided by a bullying boss.

When Natasha looks back at a situation, she wonders whether she did the right thing. "Although there were many times where I felt like my work with this human services agency was an oxymoron, things really hit rock bottom when I was yelled at for conducting research about a potential case.

"A black woman had come into our office claiming that the security guards in her local grocery store followed her around the store because of her race. When I described the situation to my supervisor, his immediate reaction was, 'Well if she's not doing anything wrong, then she shouldn't be worried about people following her.' He was a white Irish man and he could not appreciate the humiliation a person of color could feel when they were treated like a criminal while doing something as simple as food shopping. So, instead of explaining my emotional feelings with him, I decided to conduct some preliminary research on the issue, that is, whether being profiled as a shoplifter because of one's race and being followed around the store could qualify as discriminatory conduct. I wrote a brief memo supporting my instincts and I left it on his desk.

"During a weekly staff meeting, he threw the memo on the conference table and arrogantly snarled, 'I got your little memo and it's not worth the paper it's written on. I just hate to think about how much time you wasted on that crap.' (Now, we did not bill our hours so there was no financial concern about lost time.) Although I had research to support my position, he was not convinced. My fellow co-workers and I were floored when he said, 'Even in a perfect world, if a security guard admitted that he was following a customer because she was black, that's still not discriminatory.' My research clearly showed that racial profiling was discriminatory. There I was just trying to do my job, and be conscientious about it. I could not believe how he publicly berated me.

"The day after this incident, his tune changed and all of a sudden he demanded a full investigation of the complaint. He wanted undercover testers to visit the store location ASAP. You see, the head of the entire agency—a black woman—ordered him to conduct a full investigation when she learned about his statements and conduct.

"While I felt vindicated by the agency head's decision to investigate the complaint, I did not say anything to the supervisor who humiliated me and I will always regret that. I was too afraid to confront the supervisor because I feared that he would have retaliated against me. But in reality, how could he have retaliated against me? He was already making my life miserable by embarrassing me in front of my co-workers. Looking back, I should have told him that yelling at me was unacceptable and explained how belittling my work was counterproductive. My silence told this supervisor that it was ok to yell at me and treat me like the rug he wiped his feet on.

"I took a passive-aggressive approach and just stopped caring about the agency and just tried to find ways to find an escape route out of there. I started to really 'waste time' in the office by taking extended lunch breaks and taking every Friday off to find another job."

⟐ ⟐

Natasha might have greatly benefited if she had discussed the bullying incident with a close colleague in a similar profession. The internal cost-benefit analysis she conducted denied her of valuable advice and feedback for handling the situation. She didn't allow anyone into the conversation in her head, and was left with many unanswered questions.

⟐ ⟐

Jana Stephens* uses a drastically different approach when she feels like she is being bullied. Jana is a single mother with a young son. Not only does she think about her own career when she makes a decision in the workplace, but she also has to keep her son in mind. Jana has witnessed enough skirmishes in the workplace to understand that there are ways of fighting unfairness in the workplace without looking as though you are fighting. "There was an incident in a past law firm involving a female paralegal. She was on a business trip with a lawyer and they were at a hotel. She was in the hotel bar reading a book and the lawyer started talking to her. When she went up to her room, he followed her and tried to invite himself into her room. She came back and told me this. It was clearly inappropriate. But had she reported the lawyer to the firm, I don't know what action the firm would have taken and I don't know how far it would have gone. Her attitude was, 'Why bother? It's not going to be helpful to me in my career. The incident has passed, I got through it and it's not worth it for me to make a big deal.' That's really the question, when to draw the line between filing a formal complaint versus getting through these things and chalking them up to boorish behavior. You have to admire people who are willing to file lawsuits, especially women traders in investment banks. It's really extraordinary that they do it, and a lot of times there's a lot of money at stake. In terms of them being known in the industry as the person who filed a complaint, it may or may not be where you want to be career wise."

Obviously, Jana does not fight her battles on the front lines. Instead, she uses the power to influence and change behaviors one person at a time. "In a past law firm, I started working there temporarily while I was pregnant. They hired me permanently while I was six months' pregnant, which I thought was great. They had a policy of three months' paid maternity leave. But then they sent me a document asking me to acknowledge that I only got six weeks' paid maternity leave. I think I signed it but then they realized that it would not have been legal for them to do that. If they had stuck to that position, would it have been worth taking formal action to challenge them or to just say no I'm going to write off the experience? It's a tough call between what you will accept and what you will challenge. This was an instance where I spoke with some people, and as I went up the chain then people weighed in and agreed that they would give me the full three months."

⇒ ⇐

Some high-stress environments like law firms and stock market trading floors are breeding grounds for aggressive bosses and co-workers. There are employees who ignore their boss's cursing and yelling, while other employees immediately report the incident to human resources. Some people just tough it out because they feel that misconduct is a part of the office culture and will just grin and bear it. Your response will greatly depend on how you much you love the work and need the job, as well as your threshold for working in stressful environments.

CHAPTER 7

DUAL IDENTITY

How much of ourselves we display in the workplace is a serious consideration for a person in the minority, especially a visible minority. In reality, Corporate America was created by Caucasian men for Caucasian men (*Cracking the Corporate Code: The Revealing Success Stories of 32 African-American Executives*, 2003). The decorum and dress are heavily influenced by Caucasian men. So, naturally, Caucasian men have an easier time expressing various aspects of their personal identity that are not necessarily work related. For instance, it is not out of place to walk into a man's office and see a picture from his last fishing expedition, a plaque of a bass fish he caught, or the trophies from his baseball league.

We learned from the advent of casual Fridays that even most Caucasian males' office attire incorporates aspects of their personal lives. The same golf shirt or polo button-down shirt with khakis that he wore on the weekend became acceptable office attire. However, a woman wearing a bright-colored sari is sure to start a few conversations and turn a few heads in most corporate environments.

⇝ ⇜

Despite the increase in diversity programs and employee resource groups, there is still a corporate culture in most organizations that mandates a certain code of conduct that sometimes requires assimilation. Kenneth Wong,* an investment banker, looked around his office upon arrival and noticed that there were very few people in management who looked like him. This observation shaped the way he saw himself advancing within the financial center. "Not seeing any or very few managers who were people of color on my floor made me feel excluded. I mean, I saw mostly Caucasian males and a couple of Caucasian females as managing directors, vice presidents or above on my floor and probably in the company while working at this investment bank. I felt like there was a glass ceiling; that there would have to be a lot of conforming; a lot of, possibly, dilution of cultural identity in order to ascend through those ranks."

⇝ ⇜

Often, people in the minority, especially when the minority characteristic is apparent, feel as though they have to express themselves one way in the office and then another outside of the office in order to fit in with the majority culture. A 2006 article in *Essence* magazine, "How Black Can You Be? African Americans on the Job," explored this issue of dual identity. Ronald Brown, Ph.D., president of Banks Brown, a management consulting firm in San Francisco, told *Essence* magazine, "For Black women, one of the issues around corporate image has to do with the difference in hairstyles. For instance, when a woman wears dreadlocks in a corporate environment, the core message others receive is that you are probably more involved with your own culture than the corporate culture. There may be the sense that you're rejecting the very culture that's made the rest of us successful." *Essence* magazine reinforced Dr. Brown's observations by interviewing a black woman television anchor who covered her twists with a straight relaxed wig when she was on the air. The anchorwoman summed the issue up with one question when she asked, "As long as [Caucasians] have a problem with your just being here why should you give them something else to have a problem with?"

Duality involves having to negotiate how much of your culture, heritage, and personality you allow to seep into the office. For good reason, people in the minority are conscious of how they may be perceived in the workplace, especially if we are the only person with a particular characteristic. We are concerned about being stigmatized and stereotyped.

Sometimes duality involves being two drastically different people: one person at work and another at home. For instance, I had a biracial colleague who literally had two different personas, and he playfully had different names for each. He was the policy director for a non-profit organization and he worked with liberal white women who often expressed misguided generalizations about black men and the reasons for their high unemployment rates, high incarceration rates, and other societal plights. His office persona was a suave professional who wore a suit to work every day, even though his office colleagues wore jeans and sneakers to work. When he left the office, he wore a t-shirt featuring his favorite rap artist and a leather jacket with sleeves short enough to reveal the tattoos running up and down his arms. Although he felt more comfortable in casual clothes and was proud of his tattoos, which held personal significance and told his life story, he feared that his colleagues would see him as a thugged-out black man and clutch their purses as he walked by. He was concerned that his credibility as the office expert would be questioned and it would be just more difficult to get his job done. So to keep things simple, he dressed the part to play the part.

While most of us recognize the importance of exercising discretion with how much we reveal about ourselves to our managers and co-workers, it is important to analyze how the decision to leave portions of who we are out of the workplace affects how we negotiate relationships at work. While some people in the minority just accept as a fact of life that they are not going to express their personality through their style of dress, hair styles, or any other cultural indicator, others really struggle with limiting manifestations of their personalities in the workplace.

⇥ ⇤

Katrina Donaldson* felt as though she had to slip into a cultural-heritage straitjacket when she spent a summer in Mississippi working for a law firm. For six weeks that summer, she hid her personality, culture, and other minority characteristics. "It was not until I worked as a summer law clerk for an all-white law firm in Mississippi that I understood W.E.B. DuBois' concept of dual consciousness. When I first studied W.E.B. DuBois and his metaphor of 'the veil' to describe black Americans' dual identities in a majority white society, I was a college sophomore taking my first formal African-American history class. At the time, I had no context for understanding DuBois' simple principle. All my life, I had lived and learned in environments where I felt completely comfortable to be me. Most of the students in my high school were Caribbean-American, and the teachers, white and black, had the sensibilities for nurturing us. Even college, where I was sometimes the only black student in a class with 50 students, was an accepting environment to people of color. For instance, my study partner for my African-American history class was a white Jewish girl from Oklahoma, and she clung to urban culture much more than I did. She was very much aware of—and sometimes more sensitive than I to—racial disparities and inequalities in society. This was the norm for most white students I encountered on NYU's early 1990s liberal campus. I didn't realize how spoiled I was.

"I was used to working in environments where almost any look was acceptable. In one year, I went from sporting a Halle Berry bob to heavy fat braids that reached down the middle of my back. I wore trendy Timberland boots to work. I did not feel inhibited in any way. I was very comfortable when I walked through the doors of the office, whether I was coming or going.

"I got a quick wake-up call that being black meant being different during an interview for my first job with a law firm in Mississippi. Two junior white male associates took me out for coffee after my first set of morning interviews. I thought everything was going well. After a few minutes of small talk, the associates broke down and explained that I would be the firm's first black associate. Now this was not a new firm. They had been in existence since the 1800s. I couldn't believe that in 1999, I was going to become their first black associate. But even more shocking was the conversation. As the associates tried to explain their commitment to increasing diversity within the firm, I no longer felt like a qualified candidate. Instead, I felt like the black candidate. I no longer felt like one of them. I felt a division between my world and theirs. I knew that my experiences in the firm would be different than theirs. I knew that I would be seen differently and that the firm—from the partners to the support staff—would treat me as someone different. When I returned to the office for the afternoon interviews, I paid close attention to those partners, associates and support staff I met in the halls. I was conscious of how my conduct might shape these people's perception of a black associate.

"During that summer, I left much of my personality at home to keep things simple. It was hard enough convincing these old gray-haired Southern men that I was qualified to work for the firm; I didn't need any additional hurdles. I wore my hair in a bun, I dressed in safe—and drab—corporate attire and never spoke about cultural or racial issues. The last thing I wanted was for any aspect of my Caribbean identity to become office fodder. The veil had finally descended and it separated me from the firm."

⊸⊷ ⊶⊷

Sometimes the duality is forced upon us when others point out our differences. Rodney Barkley* is the typical easygoing northern California type who tries to only see one race, the human race. However, within his work environment, the cable industry, he is often nominated as the race expert on all things African-American because he is African-American. Occasionally, Rodney has to distinguish for his colleagues the difference between his opinions and those of African-Americans. He has to explain that African-Americans are not a monolithic group and each person in the race has unique and individual experiences that shape his or her world outlook, opinions, and aspirations—similar to how his majority colleagues demand to be seen as individuals.

"I've been very fortunate to work with some very good people that have never made me feel uncomfortable or feel that I was different because of my minority status. Actually, it's kind of worked in reverse. There have been instances where I have been asked questions as if I am an ambassador, if you will, when discussing the subject of race. I look at that as, well, people are naturally inquisitive and they have questions that they would like to ask and I'll be more than happy to answer. I would always preface my responses with, 'Well, I'm no ambassador for the entire African-American group. I think you'll have to go talk to them individually. But, I can share with you some of *my* experiences based on perceptions and issues that seem to have a different slant if you are a person of color versus being a Caucasian person.' But I've never, at least to my knowledge, been made to feel uncomfortable based on being a minority.

"There's two ways of looking at being involuntarily placed in the position of spokesperson. You could look at it and say, 'You're pointing me out because I am someone who is different.' But, I also think that there is an equally balanced opposite reaction. People are really interested in what I have to say as an individual. Because of my unique perspective, being a person of minority status, I provide insight into perceptions that could possibly get the person asking the question to think about what it is that they're thinking in terms of how they perceive people who are not like them. And that's how I always took that line of questioning. I never took it as a negative."

ADVICE FOR MANAGERS

One of the worst experiences one can have in the workplace is to share something personal—your culture, your life experiences, etc.—and to have someone mock you or think that you are not human—that you are an alien. With good reason people in the minority are careful as to what they reveal about themselves in the workplace. No one enjoys being embarrassed.

Identity is more than just self-expression. It is about determining how much of oneself to invest in an organization. If the organization seems to embrace people who look like you, chances are that you will stay and grow with that organization because there is, or at least appears to be, an opportunity to advance. No one wants his or her identity, the parts that are important to us, stifled. The pictures on our desk, the trophies on our walls, and the art we display are all aspects of who we are. However, if it appears that anything outside of the mainstream is accepted, then a different course of action may be taken. The grin and bear it approach kicks in. The survival mechanism is triggered. How long do you stay in an organization that does not allow you to be who you are?

During recruiting events and interviews, be honest with prospective candidates about your organization's culture. Take potential candidates on a short walk through a department so they can get a true visual of your organization—a visual that goes beyond any brochure or website.

Also, consider designing a formal process that gives candidates opportunities to learn more about your organization from people who look like them or share a similar background (e.g., school, home state). You never want to assume that a candidate wants to speak to a "fellow" minority in your organization because when you do, you risk making the person feel "othered."

The Asian candidate does not necessarily want to speak to an Asian employee to learn more about an organization. There are other aspects of the minority candidate's personality that might be more meaningful to understanding whether he or she will feel comfortable in a given work environment.

For instance, the candidate may be more interested in knowing your organization's office culture as it relates to gender and family. The candidate may even want to get a sense of the extent to which people in your department socialize at work and outside of the office. It's helpful when employers offer a range of areas about your organization that candidates can explore. Leave it up to the candidate to determine which qualities and characteristics about your firm are most important for them to pursue. The following interviewee offers a good strategy for creating more openness in recruiting:

☞ ☜

360-DEGREE INTERVIEWING: GIVING YOU AND ME AN OPPORTUNITY TO SEE IF THERE IS A FIT

"For the most part I'm a strong-willed person and I always felt like I didn't have to conform. Part of the reason why I went to my first firm was that I felt like I was given the freedom of expression and that I didn't have to adhere to any particular beliefs or whatever the firm image was. For the 5 ½ years I was at the first firm, I wore my hair braided, twisted, or in some kind of natural hairstyle. In fact the firm liked my hairstyle so much that I was featured in their brochure. I was in the firm's brochure for the longest time. The firm cared more about the quality of your work as opposed to what you looked like as long as the client was pleased with your performance.

"That's one part of the reason why I went to the firm. When I did my interviews, I wanted to go to a place where I could wear braids, where I could wear my glasses, slacks and so on. During my interviews, those were some of the questions I asked. I wanted to know whether I was free to express myself or if I had to sit in a closet and be quiet. I declined offers from places where I was told, this is not the type of place where you can express yourself. Your opinion does not count.

"When I interviewed with the firm, I met with over seven attorneys and then I came back again and then I met with three minority associates. You go through the spiel where you ask about the firm's culture and all of that. And they give you an opportunity to ask real questions. I asked the question about wearing braids. It turns out I met with an associate who had dreadlocks and I met with another associate whose hair was natural.

"In fact, I recruited heavily for the firm for several years. They consulted me on a lot of issues. They implemented a lot of my ideas. For instance, I had suggested that when minority students interview with the firm, the firm should ask which individuals they want to meet. Do they want to meet with individuals from the same school?, individuals from the same ethnic background?, the same cultural background?, and so on, to make the student candidates feel comfortable asking those questions. That became part of the protocol at the firm.

"Our recruiting department was all white. There wasn't a black person there.

"One of the things I told them was if you're a person of color, you're not going to feel comfortable saying, 'I want to speak to someone who's black.' But, if you presented the option to the candidate that they could request to speak to somebody of their own background, for instance, 'Is this something that you're interested in?' then the students are more likely to say, 'Sure. Why not?' So that was one of my ideas. I know that I was consulted regarding recruiting issues, especially when it came to bringing more minorities to the firm. But I do feel like the firm could have done more with respect to retention. In that area they were lacking. They did better and better with recruitment but then that fell off too. Every firm has its flaws, I guess.

"When I interviewed at another firm, which shall remain nameless, I phrased my question in such a way that the associate told me not to come to the firm. She did not suggest that I go to that firm. They didn't treat their minorities very well. The only reason she would suggest that I work for that firm was to practice in a particular practice area, which I won't name. Based on that, I declined the offer.

"At my second firm, it was all about the politics. You weren't allowed to be yourself. You had to be a token black person. You were there for color purposes only. You really couldn't express an opinion, especially one that was different from the norm. You couldn't dissent. You couldn't disagree with anything they had to say. It was a no-no. Even the people who were in the in-crowd could not disagree. The culture of the firm was so different.

"It's hard for me to curb my mouth. I've always felt that if you don't want to hear the answer from me, don't ask the question. In my second firm, they always asked the question. But for the most part, since no one disagreed then whatever the firm's position was went uncontested. When I came around, things were different. I was the only black person in the entire department. I was one of four black people in the NY office. The firm had more than 200 attorneys. They had a serious problem with attrition because of their policies.

"I now have my own law firm and I feel fulfilled by it because I get to call the shots. All of the organization skills I developed at my first firm have helped me tremendously in managing my business."

➬ ➬

As for asking questions, genuine interest in learning more about the next person with the aspiration of understanding is always a good idea. However, take a moment to think about how your question will be received before you ask it.

➬ ➬

For instance, Tara Philipps* had an uncomfortable encounter when a Caucasian male colleague made her hair the centerpiece of office discussion. "One time I came to work with my hair braided. A senior associate asked me in front of the secretaries and everybody, 'How do you wash that?' I answered, 'I braid it and wash it and then braid it back. What do you mean?' The associate was a man. I was offended and I wondered, how does this concern you? It's hair. I wash it. I'm clean. We weren't friends and we didn't talk about beauty secrets together, so he was not asking in that regard. He was sort of saying, 'You're different and let me point it out.' And that was my take on the situation. I don't want to be known for my cultural differences and how I want to wear my hair. I want to be thought about for good work. I don't want to be thought of as the person who is always on her own. That's the difficulty with racial discrimination. People can always find a reason to say you don't fit in. But no one is ever going to blatantly link it to race. You just conclude that you don't fit in because of cultural differences."

⇥ ⇤

Before asking questions, think about whether your questions are making someone a spectacle. Is your question too intrusive for the relationship that you have? Are you asking your question in the most sensitive way possible? If you are going to ask personal questions, try not to stereotype or ask the person questions that sound as though he or she is the ambassador for an entire group of people. For instance, if you rarely speak with a person, you really don't have the right to ask about his or her hygiene as it pertains to their hair or any other cultural display.

To make a person feel more comfortable with answering your questions, try to provide a few answers yourself. For every question you ask, you should be prepared to provide similar information about yourself. The exchange of information diffuses a situation from an interrogation into an exploratory conversation.

ADVICE FOR PROFESSIONALS AND STUDENTS

Pay close attention to the environment and the people you

meet during the interview. The interview is a mutual vetting opportunity for you and the employer. This is your chance to interview your potential employer to find out more about its ethos. Use the interview as a chance to vet the company and determine whether you would be comfortable working within that corporate culture.

BLENDING IN

Fitting in by toning down your dress is not necessarily a bad thing; you should not be afraid to fit in. However, you should have a plan for what you will do with the skills and power you acquire once you have gained access to the executive suite. If you stay in the organization, are you going to change the corporate culture by encouraging more cultural expression? How will you contribute to creating a culture in which employees of all different backgrounds feel included?

❧ ❧

Christina Hernandez,* a young corporate attorney, fit in to navigate her way through her law firm. "I felt very comfortable about my workplace. I really was. I have not experienced that discomfort. I enjoyed working with these folks who were perhaps different from me. I had the attitude that I was going to learn from them. If I needed to adapt, I would. I was not going to change who I was or anything like that. But if I needed to behave a certain way because that was the way the room behaved, that was ok with me.

"I am probably in the minority in this experience because at my first firm there were several other Asians, Hispanics, and African-Americans. Those guys left the firm before I did and I think some of them left because they did not like the environment because they felt uncomfortable. I just never felt that discomfort, I don't know why."

➤➤ ◄◄

Although we spend most hours of our days in the workplace, it is important to understand that the workplace may not be all things to us. It is not necessarily going to give you personal fulfillment or "complete you." You may not have anything in common with the people in your office. This should not frustrate you or discourage you from advancing within the organization. There is a way to strike a balance in your life.

➤➤ ◄◄

Roxanne,* a television advertising sales executive for a major television network, takes the approach that as a person of color she just wants to blend in. "For the majority of my work experience I have been the only black person. Early in my career, I was the only black person in the New York sales office of over 300 people of a prominent media company. You learn quickly to assimilate. You can be black but not too black: to further explain, more like a person who is like everyone on the team (in the office) but just happens to be black. You don't promote your blackness, your black culture, or socialize only with the other blacks (which blacks tend to do). It is easier to just do as the Romans when in Rome."

➤➤ ◄◄

Roxanne keeps her life balanced, though, by creating or joining groups that feed her cultural interests. Even though you might not be able to wear hairstyles or the clothes that express your personality, you can have a base of friends or join an organization that allows you to do so. Consider joining affinity-based professional trade organizations and social organizations where you can meet others who share your social and cultural interests. Such organizations offer camaraderie and the opportunity to discuss similar feelings about issues such as dual identity and how each person handles the situation. The relationships that you develop outside of the workplace may fill the void of not seeing or interacting with people who share your interests. As I mentioned in Chapter 2, professional trade organizations not only fill a personal interest but may also provide skill-building opportunities.

CHAPTER 8

ASSUMPTIONS, SLIGHTS, AND OTHER ANNOYANCES

There are things that annoy each one of us. Maybe it's the sound of the bathroom faucet dripping in the middle of the night. It could be the sound of your co-worker's shoes squeaking as she walks by your desk. Even worse, it might be how your client or supervisor gives you an assignment at 4:45 pm—when you didn't have anything to do all day—and wants it on her desk by the first thing the next morning. Basically, it is those little things that you sometimes cannot address in the first instance but they still get under your skin.

In the workplace, minority employees experience subtle slights and annoyances of a different flavor. We notice how we are treated differently from our majority colleagues, who may get a nicer office or a better parking space. It is noticing that in some way, your supervisor treated someone newer and less qualified, and not in your minority group, preferentially. It could also be a rude remark. It could be something so petty that you sound ridiculous complaining that it occurred.

Sometimes it is an experience that is not significant enough to complain about but it is enough to make you feel different.

ASSUMPTIONS

☞ ☜

When Betty Dominguez* worked for a financial services firm, she was initially hired as an account representative but occasionally found herself lumped in with all of the other Latina employees as a receptionist. To her bosses, whether her last name was Dominguez, Martinez, or Hernandez, it was all the same to them. Since all of the receptionists were Latina and Betty was Latina they concluded that Betty could double as a receptionist.

On more than one occasion, Betty's managers tested this flawed syllogism to her dismay. "When I was working in banking, I worked in a call center so not only did I field calls and work in financial services, but I was asked to train new employees. And then, when the secretaries of the group leaders were out—all the secretaries were Latina—I was asked to fill in for them. I have no secretarial skills. I have never been a secretary, yet out of the entire department they came to me because I was the only Latina staff person. In their minds, when the two Latina secretaries are out, they thought I should fill in. Literally, they came up to my desk and asked me to fill in for the secretaries, and I complained about it. I said I don't know why I'm being asked to do this. I have a degree in Journalism, I'm not a secretary. I'm training half the staff and I'm answering calls, and you want me to be a secretary too? And they said, 'Well, that's because you can handle the work.' That was not why.

"There were several instances where it was just assumed that I was bilingual because I have a Spanish surname. No one ever asked me if I was bilingual. It was just assumed and I was given documents to translate. I was put on the telephone with customers who did not speak English. I was just told to speak to them in Spanish without ever being asked if I was able to do that. And when I couldn't do it, or refused to do it even when I could have, it seemed as though I was being insubordinate when in fact I wasn't. I'm not fully bilingual; I'm not fluent in Spanish. I was raised in an English-speaking household. But, because of the way I look, because of my Spanish surname, the assumption was there and it was across the board at this predominantly white corporate environment.

"I complained to the group leader in my department. At that time, I was 22 years old. I was told that I was being too sensitive."

·→•◎ ◎•←·

Although we have all been subjected to assumptions and slights, people of color, women, and some employees with disabilities are greater targets because we are visibly different from our white male colleagues. It is easier to pick us out. It is easier for people to assume and determine that we do not belong. It is easier to assume that we are not qualified and to shove us into a corner. Being underestimated for no other reason than a personal characteristic is degrading. It is frustrating to be denied an opportunity to advance because you are not deemed qualified as a result of what you look like instead of how you work.

The marginalization of people who are in the minority can even happen within minority groups.

·→•◎ ◎•←·

Susan de las Cuevas* had the unique experience of encountering assumptions as a minority within a minority while working for a non-profit organization. "I felt like a minority when I worked for a predominantly black organization and I was one of the only Latino staff people in the organization.

"I felt like a minority in that instance because as a Latina I became, not because I chose to, but by virtue of the fact of the small number of Latinos in the organization, a spokesperson for an ethnic group. As a result of that, I never experienced feeling 'othered' the way that I did in that organization. I was assumed to be bilingual because I was Latina. I was reminded on various occasions that I was not African-American.

I was siloed into a role where my goals were really based on my background as an ethnic person and not my academic or professional credentials. For example, I was given many opportunities in the organization but when promotions came they gave me a title that had to do with working with a Latino contingency. And I felt that because I was Latino, they just assumed that I was othered because I was not African-American—not knowing my upbringing, not knowing where I grew up, not knowing my family background, not knowing my interest or my history. The assumption was that, you are not African-American.

"And because we were all people of color, the bifurcation was clear. It wasn't subtle. When you work in a white environment, people are very careful not to say comments that can be seen as racist. But when you're working in an environment that is predominantly people of color, those kind of subtleties are thrown out the window because you don't have to be so careful. I felt like a minority and I was a minority in that environment. I was treated as a minority in that environment and I was made to feel othered because I didn't share the predominant ancestry of the majority—African-Americans.

"Here's an example of how I was othered. I was at a staff breakfast and I was told when I walked into the dining space by an African-American colleague that they were not serving rice and beans for breakfast and asked if I was still hungry.

"On another occasion, at a national staff conference in Las Vegas, I was asked if I could translate something for the table that was in Spanish. When I said that I was not able to translate, I was told that I wasn't a real Latina because I couldn't speak Spanish. I was so hurt and offended and embarrassed by that comment because it was said at a table with people I didn't know. I actually ran out of the room crying and I didn't go back that evening until much later. The other thing that happened at the staff conference, the same colleague said in front of everybody, 'Well, we can't ask Susan* because she's never left the Bronx.' And then another colleague came to my defense and said, 'Well actually, she has lived in London and in Spain, and she has lived all over the United States. Did you know that?' And again, the assumption is because I'm a Puerto Rican woman born and raised in the Bronx, the assumption is that I've never left this environment, which is not true."

⇢⇒ ⇐⇠

SLIGHTS

Subtle slights and small actions may seem minuscule, but they accumulate. After a while, they build and may erode employee-employer relationships and eventually cause minority employees to lose their loyalty to the organization.

⇢⇒ ⇐⇠

Kea Jamison* left a promising career as a lawyer because of the accumulation of subtle slights including being left out of meetings. "Every Monday morning I knew what to expect when I walked into the office. The partner who gave me and the other associate our assignments would be in a meeting with Isaac,* a young junior associate, to discuss his caseload. The meetings usually lasted an hour and were held behind a closed door. Sometimes I would hear laughter seep through the doors. When the meeting was over, they would leave the conference room together as though they were old buddies. Isaac walked out of each meeting knowing what the partner expected of him for the week. Isaac knew his responsibilities and had a clear direction for the rest of the week, thanks to the assigning partner.

"I was never invited to these meetings, and I resented feeling left out. 'Why would I be upset when Isaac had his meetings?' you are probably asking. Didn't I have my own meetings? Although I asked for a weekly meeting similar to Isaac's, I didn't have the same quality of meetings as Isaac. For a couple of weeks, the partner carved out 20 minutes to meet with me. But then each week, the partner would ask if we could reschedule. Eventually, the meetings were permanently postponed.

"Each week as I struggled to juggle a full caseload, on my own, I would have flashbacks of watching Isaac and the partner hamming it up. This partner, who rarely gave me assignments face-to-face, had an entire hour to devote to Isaac. When I spoke with Isaac about how those meetings made me feel excluded, Isaac would always say that the meetings were no big deal. The partner and Isaac were white men, while I was the lone black woman associate. Why didn't the partner make time to meet with me?

"To allay my concerns, Isaac would describe the meetings as 'punitive.' By trivializing the meetings, he made me sound as though I had blown things out of proportion. But I didn't. Maybe the Monday case meetings, per se, were not a big deal, but combined with the absence of mentoring and support, they were unbearable to watch and experience.

"After a while, those Monday meetings were like a cavity and they rotted every aspect of my work experience. Because the partner would not have case review meetings with me and was usually unavailable, I was left to figure out everything on my own. Instead of asking the partner a question where I could get an answer in five minutes, I would spend an hour researching the answers.

"The partner's small slight of not meeting with me at least once a week like he did with Isaac had a detrimental effect on my work and my ability to contribute to the office. I started to lose confidence in my work and in my abilities. When the U.S. Supreme Court decided the *Burlington Northern & Santa Fe Railway v. White* case in 2006, I felt vindicated. Although this case was a retaliation case, our nation's highest court recognized that when a boss extends an invitation to take some members to lunch and not others, especially when mentoring and training are involved, he could hinder the excluded employee's professional development. Each Monday that I watched Isaac meet with the assigning partner, I was denied mentoring and training."

→◉ ◉←

OTHER ANNOYANCES

→◉ ◉←

Felix Johansson* is an African-American television anchorman in the Midwest. The subtleties in his colleagues' and supervisor's interaction with him involve a constant struggle for respect. While his white male colleagues are given wide latitude with what they say and how they say it, Felix knows that he must be more careful to avoid any stereotypes of being the newsroom's angry black man.

"I feel like if I get upset about something, people immediately say that I'm giving them attitude. When another person feels strongly about something, they're passionate.

"One day this reporter who does not come up with good stories came up with the idea of covering whether business was going well for retailers during the holiday season. Now, who couldn't come up with that story? What a lame story. You can do that story anytime. She doesn't work hard to get good stories. I work hard to pitch good stories.

"Last week she pitched a story about how gas prices are up. The assistant news director said, well we've done that story, what else can we do about this story. Later in the meeting, all of a sudden it turned into a good story for *me* to do. I asked why it was a good story for me to do and suggested that the person who pitched the story cover it. After the meeting, I said, again, that I did not want to do a story about gas prices because the story I pitched was better. I pitched a story about how local churches were building homes and shipping them to Louisiana. We should do a story that affects our community. The news editor told me that I did not have to cover the story. The assistant news editor, however, said, 'If it was up to me, you would be covering the gas prices story.' I asked why? She then asked why I was giving her attitude. I spoke to her privately and reminded her that I put 100% into everything that I do.

"I told her that as a black male I'm perceived to have an attitude if I don't agree with something in the workplace. She then accused me of playing the race card. I told her that I wasn't playing the race card. There is another reporter, a white male in his 50s and he's been in this market for 20 years. Sometimes, the reporters will pitch a story and he'll say, 'That's a bunch of bullshit. I'm not doing this story. It's stupid.' This reporter will even step out of the camera if there is a live shot at the last minute. He won't do it, and he's right. You should never do anything that makes you look bad on-air. He does this all the time. Why is it when he objects to doing a story, it's ok. It's brushed off as Joe* is just being Joe. But when I say that I don't want to do a story, I'm giving everyone attitude. The assistant news editor said, 'That's because he makes his objections and moves on.' I said he moves on because he doesn't do the stories he doesn't want to do. She went on to justify his behavior by saying, 'He's been in this market for a long time.' I explained to her that it doesn't matter. Covering stories is his job. I explained that there was a double standard.

"If I was younger, I would let this eat me up. I would come home and be in a bad mood and take my anger out on people around me. I would come to work with a bad attitude and a chip on my shoulder. I just remember to do the best that I can and to have a positive attitude. I go to a good church with a progressive ministry and I'm just reminded about how blessed I am. I read over my notes from church and remind myself to not let people steal my joy. I know better so I'm always going to smile. I still have to say that I have a great job."

➻ ➺

ADVICE FOR MANAGERS

Subtle slights, annoyances, and assumptions are unnecessarily dangerous to an organization because they often lead to claims of discrimination and harassment in addition to making employees feel excluded. Frequently, employment discrimination cases can be sparked by the smallest instance of insensitive behavior. The Equal Employment Opportunity Commission, which enforces federal anti-discrimination laws in the workplace, receives over 70,000 complaints each year.

As a former employment lawyer representing employees against management, I can assure you that many of those complaints were the result of subtle slights and annoyances. For instance, I once had an African-American client, we'll call him

John, who felt that his termination was racially motivated. He distrusted his employer and did not believe that he was laid off because his position was eliminated. Instead, he believed that his boss was a racist. Why? Because, the boss, a white male, would not say "hello" to him, while he would greet all of the other employees, who happened to be white.

When a supervisor fails to extend the same treatment, especially respect and courtesy, to all employees, the slighted minority employee may feel the sting of exclusion. Although an organization may feel that their corporate goodwill overcomes slights and annoyances, think again. Given that our memories of negative experiences are more accurate than our memories of positive events, according to a 2006 Harvard study, your employees are more likely to remember a rude remark or the failure to say "hello" much better than they remember the company outing.

Although it seems like common sense that managers should know better than to treat their minority employees like second-class citizens, it happens. As the 21st-century adage about diversity in the workplace goes, "Companies get diversity; it's their managers who don't." For proof of this schism, just look at any company that is recognized for its diversity efforts. I guarantee that you will find that the same company has employees who lodged discrimination complaints because of a manager's misconduct or failure to address misconduct. Often, employees of the companies that received awards for their diversity practices doubt that their company was worthy of recognition.

CONCRETE STEPS

Often, when we talk about diversity and specifically respect in the workplace, it is in abstract concepts. Managers are told to "value" their employees, "develop" their skills, and "motivate" their workforce. However, managers are rarely given a road map to figuring out how to achieve these goals with concrete steps.

→● ●←

Stephanie Murray's* experiences give managers a rare glimpse of what types of conduct and behavior have negative effects on their workforce. "Subtle adversity requires people of color to endure extra, unnecessary steps that the majority does not face. I've had numerous discussions with various individuals (women or people of color) who have faced various types of adversity where they felt marginalized by the 'majority's' actions. Adverse actions based upon discriminatory factors prompt me to step up to the plate even more to ensure that I do not yield power to the majority or anyone who does not have my best interest in mind.

"You can't and would not want to flee from being a woman, a person of color, or a youthful-looking individual. These factors are especially relevant when the people in executive or leading roles are primarily much older, white, or male. Many of the adverse situations I have faced involved situations where I had to fight for a leadership role or to work on a high-profile project.

For example, a Caucasian deponent walked out of a deposition room after learning I was not an observer in the room but the attorney who was taking the deposition. My Caucasian colleagues uneasily smirked and took no actions. A definitive answer will never exist as to whether the deponent thought, 'Oh, she's 1) too young or 2) just a silly woman or 3) just that person of color, who didn't get it and is not going to waste my time.' But, one can logically deduce the deponent's thoughts fell into one of the three categories since we had not previously met or spoken.

"Under this and similar circumstances, I focus(ed) on what I need(ed) to do to prove myself to myself and how I could/can maximize upon the adverse situation. Once I reminded the deponent that he was under a subpoena to return to the room for the deposition and he did so reluctantly, I seized the opportunity to acknowledge within myself that the deponent's adverse actions were of no moment to my success, and, as an irrelevant byproduct, to prove each of the deponent's 'unspoken assumptions' wrong. I focused on what I learned about the deponent from his documents and actions so that I could gather the information I needed from the situation.

"This situation is very analogous to today's subtle adversity; it's in the way that certain individuals might talk to or at you like you're a two-year-old or call you endearing names (e.g., girl, darling, sweetie, son, etc.) or use colloquial terms (e.g., my bad, whassup, etc.) when you are supposed to be conducting business and you do not have a personal relationship.

"Analogous to my tactics in the deposition, I figure I'm going to wear such adverse individuals down and make them so tired until they give me the relevant information I need to succeed in a given situation. For example, in the deposition, I asked so many different questions in so many different ways that neither the deponent nor his attorney could keep track. By the end of the deposition, the deponent started to respect me and ignore his attorney. Similarly, in work situations, I will assert myself in situations where I am notably excluded if it will benefit my mission where feasible. These tactics, which are tiring, will not always work, but I recognize that it is my best interest to be flexible enough to switch them for each given situation to yield the most beneficial professional and personal goals for myself and other people of color."

Employers should be mindful of their stereotypes and assumptions. Employees are people with individual personalities, likes, and dislikes.

Generations X and Y, especially, pride themselves in believing that we are special. To lump us together because of the way we look, act, or sound is like cyanide to our souls. Even worse is generalizing about us because of our race, ethnicity, or other characteristics. We resent when we do not have the opportunity to make our own mark in an organization. Plus, it's tiring having to live in the shadows of an antiquated boss's definitions of a woman or a person of color. It is tiring working for a boss who cannot see us as people.

↦ ↤

Lalia Bhindra* was the only Asian attorney and one of two women of color in her law firm. After a few similar encounters of mistaken identity, she started to feel as though she was not seen as or treated as a person but instead a color. "It was bizarre how people confused me with the other associate of color. I would send an email and ask for something or she would send an email and then all of a sudden someone would walk into her office and say, 'Hey, you know that email you sent...' and she would be like, I have no idea of what you are talking about. And then the person would realize it was me. It's like, are you kidding?"

↦ ↤

Advice for Professionals and Students

While your antennae should be sensitive to disparate treatment, I caution you against taking every comment or action too seriously. Try to focus on solutions to the problem and not someone's stupidity. Remember, sometimes our perceptions are not necessarily the objective reality. You don't want to cry wolf that you were discriminated against by someone who is an equal opportunity jerk. This diminishes your credibility as someone with good judgment who should be taken seriously. You will need this credibility if and when something truly egregious occurs.

John, the client I mentioned above, who brought the discrimination case because his boss would not say hello to him, wasted a lot of money and time because he was overly sensitive. While it was rude of his employer not to extend the common courtesy of "hello," John didn't realize that anti-discrimination laws are not civility codes. The laws do not protect against trivial slights and annoyances, per se.

A good strategy for testing the frequency of your antennae is having a group of colleagues and advisors who exercise good judgment and can keep your confidences. Before you allow a petty situation to ruin your work environment, ask your cadre of advisors for their thoughts. Depending on their expertise level, you should gather their advice for handling the situation. John's circle should have suggested that he find other ways to test whether his supervisor's racist tendencies were adversely affecting his employment or whether the supervisor was just inconsiderate.

He could have tried to put his supervisor in a position where he had to speak to him by asking questions related to a project or something very important in the workplace. Now, if the supervisor still did not speak to John, John would have a serious situation on his hands. His supervisor was not merely withholding salutations, but he would be affecting John's ability to do his job. If John was the only person of color in the department, and he was the only person the supervisor did not speak to and advise, then John had clearer circumstances of inequality and could show a lack of opportunity and fairness in the workplace. He would have had a clearer case of discrimination. John would have had more evidence and information to make a serious complaint.

Ultimately, employees who stay focused on the big picture don't get tripped up by subtle slights, assumptions, and other annoyances. When someone shows how in the dark they are about who you are, use it to your advantage. Don't get mad, get smart.

➤➤ ➤➤

Paris* was a rising talent in her media firm. However, her supervisor thought that she was too young to get a particular promotion. Instead of getting angry, she turned the tables on his perceptions of youth.

"I was up for a promotion from manager to director, but the new president of my division thought I was too young to be a director. (I was in my mid twenties but I have a youthful face.) He didn't give my boss the approval and told my boss that he thought I was too young, and that I needed to be more seasoned.

"Two weeks later at the company Christmas party the new president stopped to talk to me. He said, 'I think you are around my daughter's age.' I said, 'Oh?' He said, 'She's in her early 30s.' I said with a smile, 'Oh you're right. She is,' knowing that I was only 27.

"My promotion was approved the next day."

CHAPTER 9

BEING THE FIRST AND NOT HAVING AN EXTENSIVE NETWORK

I have a friend—I'll call him Albert—who is incredibly smart and has great interpersonal skills. He graduated from top-notch undergraduate and graduate schools and has worked for competitive companies. In essence, Albert, professionally, has it going on.

However, during a recent conversation with Albert, he explained the daunting complexities of advancing within his company that had nothing to do with merit or talent.

He told me a story about a woman in his office who asked a senior-level executive for business development advice. She knocked on the executive's door, sat down, and proceeded to ask the senior executive how he finds new business opportunities and generates million-dollar accounts for the company. She was curious about how he met and attracted the business of high-caliber clients. The executive reached into his desk for a magazine. He pointed to the front cover of a business magazine and explained that his relative, who was pictured next to a few well-known CEOs of Fortune 500s, creates introductions and entrees for him. This executive reached the highest level of success in this organization because he was able to pick up the telephone and ask his aunt to introduce him to any CEO he wanted to meet. What an enviable position!

Although Albert is bright, charismatic, personable, and courageous, he explained that as an African-American male, his challenges to developing business were two tiered. First, he did not feel welcomed enough by the executive or any of the white male executives in his office such that he could knock on their door to have a conversation about business development. Albert did not feel that he had the same access to a white male executive as his white female colleague. He strongly doubted whether the executive would be as open with him about business development.

His second barrier to creating business the way the executive did was that he does not have an aunt or uncle with multimillion-dollar business connections. Albert is the first person to work in a profession where he has to generate clients. So despite his hard work, Albert is forced to find other ways to demonstrate his value to his company because he does not have multimillion-dollar connections at his finger tips.

Albert's experience is not uncommon for people in the minority who are the first in their families. Whether we are the first in our families to graduate from college, the first to pursue a career that requires an advanced degree, or the first generation to live in the United States, we realize how not having lucrative business networks creates additional hurdles in the way of our advancement.

Many of us realize that there is a point in our careers where our hard work will not get us as far as advantageous connections. We observe how our counterparts in the majority often have an expansive network that works overtime for them. These networks, which are often created by their parents, get them into the best boarding schools, colleges, and companies. And once they are in these institutions, they have someone looking out for them. They have someone who cares about their development and their image and will steer them toward the best projects that will give them the best experience and best exposure. This is very powerful.

Unlike our majority colleagues, we often do not have anyone who is senior level enough to make a telephone call on our behalf to recommend us for a position or convince a potential employer to meet with us for an interview. (Sometimes, even when we have connections we don't know how to use them to open up doors for us.) To not have an extensive business network is like showing up to play in the major leagues but still having a T-ball bat.

❧

Sylvia Hong* understands all too well what it feels like to be denied access to a business network. "There's always a male club or a white club. When I was a partner in one of the large global New York firms, every partner had a III or IV after his name. There weren't too many female partners. The women partners usually worked harder and they didn't come from the same background as the men. Unless you went to prep school, or had that type of family lineage—although you made partner—you were not part of the club. You didn't belong to the country club, you didn't go to prep school, you didn't go to Choate, you didn't go to Exeter, etc. You are always an outsider. It's always, they're entitled. It's their call as to how high you achieve in their game. You are not one of them. You're not invited to the same social gatherings; you don't have the same social background necessarily. You're not one of them. You never will be.

"For the male side you weren't one of the guys unless you were into sports and other guy things. You don't get invited to do the social things, the after-work things where people continue to talk business. They had their own social circles. They would get together but I would never get invited. It made me feel like I wasn't one of them. Am I any different? No.

"I left the firm in part because of this exclusion. No matter how hard I tried or how well I did, I was never going to be good enough to overcome that. And this was in every firm I worked at. Even in the government, if you're at the top you're either in the club or you're not. People generally hire alike.

"You have to want the diversity if you want to buck the trend. It's like the studies show, that if you have more 'African-American sounding first names' that are different than Michael or Jennifer, people look at the resumes differently. I just think that there are not many differences in firms or corporations unless they are global corporations where their business is driven globally, like a PepsiCo or Coke. But if they're not driven globally, if they don't have people from global groups, then it's not going to happen."

⇢⥇⊙　⊙⥇⤙

As the first, minorities often create their own paths by walking. We are the first in our families or group of friends to work in high-level professional environments. We are sometimes the first to sit at the same tables with dignitaries and other very important people you normally see on television. Sometimes, we're the ones on television. We have neither family members who are in-the-home role models nor sources of information about how to develop business strategies, deal with a conniving supervisor, negotiate salary, or any of the other higher-tiered maladies of the workplace. We have to go it alone. Just when we thought that that our Master's, Juris Doctor, or Doctor of Medicine degree was making life easier, the ride has just begun.

When Keith Clarkson* looks back to the earlier days of his career, he quickly runs out of fingers to count the number of mistakes and missteps he made. Keith finally made it to the partnership ranks of his firm, but it was a struggle. Even as a white male, he felt left out of influential socioeconomic networks that could have assisted him in his career. "I grew up lower middle class in a small suburb of Cleveland and nobody else on either side of my family was an attorney. Even though my dad was a school superintendent and had a Ph.D. in education and I had one uncle who had a Ph.D. and was a professor of biology, no one else in my family had graduate degrees. From the standpoint of having input, and models and familiarity with what attorneys do, what career paths, what credentials matter, how to network, how to draw business, and any of that stuff, I did not have a built-in model from my upbringing. I went to New York University School of Law, which had a pretty good career services counseling division, but I still didn't feel like I learned and understood a lot of things that I believe people with a different upbringing would naturally know. If I had had such a background, I might have made wiser choices that would have increased my flexibility earlier in my career.

"In terms of interviewing, developing mentoring relationships and things like that, my perception is that people generally subconsciously find it easier to relate to people who share more characteristics with them. While I did not feel like I had as acute of a set of differences in my background—the way I talked, the way I dressed and my understanding of things and my interests—as people with legally protected characteristics, I had enough of a difference that there were instances that I felt caused me to not get the job or to not be mentored as much as someone else, etc.

"Now that I am on the flipside of the situation and in a position to mentor others, I try to make sure that I'm not limiting the extent to which I extend myself and recognize capability and encourage development in other people based on focusing on my ability to feel comfortable with them given my own unique set of things that make me who I am.

"I've never had anything horrible happen to me. I feel like everyone, except the ultra privileged, has felt like outsiders at times and sometimes it has adversely affected them because of people's tendency to fall back on going with what is most familiar and comfortable to them."

⇥ ⇤

Being the first increases the chances of being blind-sided by new experiences both substantive and interpersonal. In addition to being the first in her family to become a doctor, Barbara Tomlinson* has to figure out how to do her job without the support of her colleagues.

She works in a hospital that is a community hospital affiliate of a prestigious university. This is the first time where she is working in an institution where the staff is comprised of ethnic and racial minorities to the point where Caucasians may be in the numerical minority in her department. Yet she still feels like an outsider in many instances. She is one of the youngest attendings on staff, so she is a minority in terms of her age. In terms of experience, this is her third year out of residency, so she is essentially the third least experienced physician on staff. "I find that, particularly, when I interact with surgeons I feel like an outsider. There have been many instances where I am not invited to join in on the camaraderie that exists between some of the more established attendings and surgeons. I'm essentially not invited to participate in that arena. It's like my focus is basically to come in and do the job that I was hired to do. The interactions that occur within the hospital setting tend to be about business with me while they tend to be more social chit-chat when occurring amongst other people. I don't know if the socializing extends outside of work, because if it does then I am totally unaware of it. That is how out of the loop I am."

⟶⟞◎ ◎⟝⟵

Being the first also means learning on the job how to strategically maneuver within management's complex dynamics. The path to partnership and the executive suite is fraught with fragile egos, pettiness, and politics. Within even the most transparent workplace networks, there are power dynamics and a culture of respecting the power dynamic. Those who are outside of the workplace network often do not know the unwritten rules and protocol of how to navigate the network. These are the skills business, law, and engineering schools do not teach. Ambitious professionals like Carter Jefferson* learn through painful trial and error how to respect the power dynamic's elusive culture.

⟶⟞◎ ◎⟝⟵

Carter works for an international media company and he recently had his first encounter with the power dynamic. "A great example of what's going on in my current job is who's on the leadership track and who's not. And it's a little bit hot and cold. Now it's about not hearing about things. Like, all of a sudden someone is in a new role and you never even knew about it. No one pulled you to the side and gave you the opportunity to consider it.

"Someone from corporate had put my name in the hat for a leadership program at a historically black college where I would be an adjunct faculty person for a day. It was a part of a broader initiative. They sent me this formal letter and asked me to consider it. I was excited about it. I decided to forward the information to my boss and my boss's boss and let them know that I was chosen by the executive team to do this. There was zero response via email. So my wheels are turning.

"What ended up happening was that I ran into the person from corporate who sent me the email and he said that he had his hand slapped the other day. I said what you are talking about. He said, I had selected you because you've done a lot of things for corporate. You've spoken on panels and done a lot of things. But the head of human resources (HR) for my division contacted the HR person in corporate and said, 'I pick my people, you don't pick my people. So if you want someone from my division in on that leadership program, I pick those people; you don't.' So it was a power play.

"Once again, it's an issue of who is in your inner circle and who is not. I didn't get the nod from the head of HR from my division because I had not befriended that person. There are favorites. There are people who are picked for the short list for leadership development and for visible projects at any organization. And the favorites tend to get shaped by what's familiar, like who you hang out with, etc. It's not from a meritocracy standpoint.

"Who is in your inner circle? You take care of the folks who are around you. Sometimes we have to extend ourselves, in unreasonable ways, to become a part of the network, but it doesn't mean that we are a part of the network in a real way. It's a chess game. First you have to exhibit the ability to perform. Then you have to send the signal that your skills are valuable to the organization and if the organization does not do the right thing, then you have to create other options that are more stimulating and attractive."

⤙⊙ ⊙⤚

ADVICE FOR MANAGERS

The college model for acclimating minority students who are the first to attend college in their families presents much food for thought for corporations and firms. Anyone who has been to college knows that there is more to college than homework. At four-year colleges, students who are the first in their families to attend college are twice as likely as their counterparts who have at least one parent with a bachelor's degree to drop out of college by their first year (Choy, 2001).[2] Although many first-generation college students are smart, articulate, and have the potential to become successful, many drop out of college because they are less prepared for the college environment and have difficulty acclimating. There are peer networks, study groups, financial aid, and other dynamics that can heavily weigh on whether a person will be successful.

Intervention programs such as Upward Bound and Posse work with students from underserved communities to familiarize them with college and its processes, which can seem esoteric to outsiders. Through one-on-one counseling, personal outreach, and seminars with guest speakers, these programs improve the graduation rates for students who are the first.

The same concept of having emotional and political support in college applies to the workplace, and managers can play a pivotal role. As I mentioned in Chapter 1: Absence of Informal Mentoring, it is a good idea for your organization to strongly consider creating formal mentoring programs. Mentors help employees integrate into the workplace and help them develop meaningful relationships. They provide a

---

[2] Choy, Susan P. 2001. *Students Whose Parents Did Not Go to College: Postsecondary Access, Persistence, and Attainment* (NCES 2001-126). Washington, DC: U.S. Department of Education, National Center for Education Statistics. http://nces.ed.gov/pubs2001/2001126.pdf.

human connection, which is often ignored or overlooked in the workplace. Connecting to other people at work is just as important as connecting with people in our personal lives. In fact, there are small business owners who went back to corporate life in part because they could not handle the solitude of being a one-person show.

As people, we do not shelve our emotions and feelings the moment we walk into the workplace. Certainly, in a professional environment we don't display all of our personal baggage; however, we're still carrying it. Mentors make it possible for employees to focus on work-related issues because they are there to listen to an employee's concerns and help them find solutions. Mentors also make it possible to create a team-focused environment by explaining office nuances. By chipping away at an employee's uncertainty about the way things *really work,* a mentor can increase an employee's ability to focus on performance and productivity.

Often, managers erect barriers to networks or the "in-crowd" by selectively choosing some employees over others to participate in mentoring programs or leadership training. Organizations should have objective criteria for selecting employees for training opportunities. This way, any employee can clearly determine whether the participants in a training program were chosen fairly and whether they met the standards for participation. Employees will also know how they need to improve and work toward participating in the programs that will further their careers. Managers should try their best to remove any indications of favoritism.

Organizations often make the mistake of assuming that their affinity groups will effectively create office networks and therefore leave these groups to run on automatic pilot. Similar to any other business initiative, diversity requires action. Harvard Professor Frank Dobbins' research, "Best Practices or Best Guesses? Assessing the Efficacy of Corporate Affirmative Action and Diversity Policies," revealed that affinity groups more often than not fail to create meaningful networks for minority employees and do not advance diversity because they are comprised of junior-level employees with minimal experience with and influence over the organization. Senior-level employees should receive incentives and other support for their participation in and leadership of affinity groups to ensure that they are recognized the same way in which they would get credit for furthering any other organizational business initiative. Affinity groups that focus on career management, leadership skills building, and the other tools needed to become effective leaders have the potential to create the networks that minority employees need.

ADVICE FOR PROFESSIONALS AND STUDENTS

Regardless of your company's formal mentoring program, corporate university, or any other leadership program, your career development is your responsibility. It is up to you to take charge of where you want to go and how you are going to get there.

The first step for gaining access to a network is to be a stellar performer. When your work speaks for itself, others will recognize you and want to learn more about you.

Try not to take it personally if you are not tapped for an opportunity. Consider a strategy for finding any gaps in your performance by asking your manager, calmly, for feedback about your work. Also, try to cozy up to the individuals your manager perceives as "star" performers. There's nothing wrong with observing their work styles or asking them for pointers. Can you think of a better person to emulate than the employee your manager admires?

You should also devote a percentage of your time to networking and meeting more people. Obviously, the more people you know, the more access you have to information, resources, and opportunities. Networking is a two-way street. The worst networkers are the people who only promote themselves and do not think about how they can help others. Just think, do you enjoy being in a conversation with someone who only talks about him- or herself? Try to start the conversation by asking what the next person does, and really listen and seem interested. The more you know about the next person, the better positioned you are to figure out how you fit within each other's lives.

Once you actually make connections with new people, you need to follow up. One of my favorite business principles from *Nice Girls Don't Get the Corner Office: 101 Unconscious Mistakes Women Make That Sabotage Their Careers* (Lois P. Frankel, 2005) is, "When you need that relationship, it's already too late to build it." I'll admit, when I was a law student I found the follow-up aspect of networking challenging. I was good at meeting people, carrying on a great conversation and then it would end there. I would get caught up with a paper for school and would forget to email or send the person I met a "nice to meet you" card.

Here's a good example of how I cheated myself of a friendship with a U.S. senator. When I was in law school, an unassuming affable attorney conducted a mock interview session with me. We had a productive session as he coached me through answering questions to any future employer's satisfaction. He encouraged me to keep in touch. Well, between looking for a summer clerkship and trying to keep up with reading for class, I never followed up. I didn't send a thank-you note or an email after the mock interview session. Six months later, I picked up my Sunday newspaper and learned that this unassuming attorney, David Vitter, was running for the Senate. I was elated when he won, but I couldn't resist the urge to kick myself for not staying in touch.

Meeting new people and creating meaningful new relationships takes practice and time. You may have to meet some people a few times before you actually click. With mobile device technologies like cell phones and PDAs, you have no excuse for not staying in touch. Many times, I will send someone I just met a quick email when I am on the train or I will immediately schedule a telephone call with a person I want to meet with for lunch. Today, I designate at least 30% of my time to meeting and keeping in touch with the people I meet. Truly, there is no point in collecting cards and having thousands of people in your rolodex if you are not going to use this information wisely.

One of my favorite training programs that I present to professional trade organizations, such as the National Black M.B.A.'s, is "Finding Your Office Rabbi." While mentors can assist with procedural and substantive work-related issues, rabbis are a whole other area of support. Rabbis in Judaism are more than spiritual leaders. Since they know everyone in the congregation, they are great sources of information. They know about real estate, they know about financial investments, and they even know who is single and make for great matchmakers. Rabbis provide resources that help their congregants navigate through life's most tricky areas.

Similarly, a workplace rabbi is just as pivotal to one's workplace success. More than a mentor, a rabbi can open doors when merit and hard work can not. They advocate for you when you are not present in meetings. They mention your work to important people. And they introduce you to the people you need to know.

A great example of how important it is to have someone

looking out for you was presented in a *New York Times* article, "Under 40, Successful, and Itching for a New Career." The article featured an attractive blonde woman who was able to move from Omaha, Nebraska, to New York, land a great job, attend parties where she could meet partners of major New York City law firms, and get set up on a blind date with an oncologist because she had a rabbi. Her rabbi introduced her to a network of people who cared about her personal and professional well-being. Within a year, she had access to privileged circles that most people who spend their entire lives in New York do not have.

CHAPTER 10

ISOLATION AND BEING IGNORED

→══ ══←

"I am invisible, understand, simply because people refuse to see me. Like the bodiless heads you see sometimes in circus sideshows, it is as though I have been surrounded by mirrors of hard, distorting glass. When they approach me they see only my surroundings, themselves, or figments of their imagination—indeed, everything and anything except me."

Ralph Ellison, *Invisible Man*

→══ ══←

With all the talk about diversity, the reality is that when you get to the executive or the most senior levels of management, there is very little diversity. In a report about 94 Fortune 1000 government contractors, the U.S. Department of Labor found that while minorities and women, respectively, make up 15.5% and 37.9% of the total workforce, they occupy only 6% and 16.9% of the management positions. At the executive level, only 3.6% are minority and 6.6% women.

There are a myriad of reasons to explain the dearth of women and minorities in management positions. By the time professionals who were the "only one" could have advanced to senior management, many have left because of the horrible experiences of being excluded. Some leave because they grew tired of watching others with fewer qualifications get the better assignments or they grew tired of getting edged out for promotions. Even worse, some were asked to leave.

An aspect of being a person in the minority is being and feeling alone. Because you do not have any or many others who share important characteristics with you, you can feel ostracized from conversations and not privy to the collegiality of the group.

Sometimes those in the majority are so unfamiliar with "your type" that they do not know how to relate to you. Many people are not curious or courageous enough to leave their comfort zones to find out about someone who they suspect is different from them. Some people in the majority are afraid that they may say or do something offensive. Some may just assume that they have nothing in common with a person in the minority and thus nothing to say. It is not uncommon for those in the majority to do what feels easy and comfortable: socialize with the people who look like and act like them.

⇥ ⇤

Raheema Strickland* was a young black associate in a law firm with 1,000 lawyers worldwide and a handful of associates of color when she had to leap out of her comfort zone. She was often the only brown face in a room and the only voice of color in a conversation. Something as simple as starting and joining a conversation was a challenge for Raheema because she was one of a very few people with her background and experience.

"When I was a summer associate at a large New York City

law firm I felt like sometimes when you would get in conversations with people, either groups of other lawyers or groups of
other partners and summer associates where they would start
talking about something, I had no relation to them. I don't
know if it was class or race. I can't clearly identify what it was. It
just seemed like we had very different experiences. Whatever it
was that they were discussing, I just didn't feel like I could contribute to the conversation. So I would just find another group
of people to talk to. After a while, I started inserting whatever
my experiences or opinions were even if I couldn't relate to what
they were talking about."

Raheema knew that she could not afford to be a quiet
minority in her firm. She had to find a way to display her gre-
garious personality and be a visible part of the group. Why?
She needed to emerge from the shadows of her majority colleagues. She wanted, and needed, the law firm partners to
keep her in sight and in their minds when they were assigning
high-level and challenging projects to associates.

Being the "only one" increases the chances of feeling invisible. When we are not the first to be considered for projects
that will enhance our skills and background, as the "only ones"
it is not difficult to feel excluded. When our managers do not
consider us for projects and we are only an afterthought, we
wonder whether our managers even see us at all. You notice
being singled out in big and small ways.

Kahleel Faroud* saw his career in the financial services
industry slipping off-track when he was hired as the first and
only Muslim to work on a particular team for an investment
banking firm. The novelty of being the first had consequences

Kahleel did not anticipate. "I felt like I was the only person of color when I worked in private banking. The person who hired me did not treat me any different than my co-workers. The team that I was placed on, well, I felt a little bit outside of my comfort zone.

"We had different ethnicities and at the same time different religious beliefs as well. Although we didn't speak about it, there were other team members that shared the same ethnicities and the same religious backgrounds and I just felt like they bonded more so with each other than with me. I just didn't feel comfortable in terms of asking questions or being invited to certain outings. I'm Muslim and these gentlemen were Jewish. They were pro-Israel and I am from Afghanistan.

"In the beginning when I was hired what was unique was that they invited me to join the team, but once I joined the team I noticed that I wasn't being trained. That was a little bit strange to me. I don't know what the dynamics or the selection criteria were for the group to invite me to the team and then not give me the resources and training to be successful. There was a training program. After you obtain your licenses, you are absorbed into a private wealth team.

"Usually, you shadow the senior wealth managers on client calls at various meetings. The only client call that I ever attended was a lead that I was able to bring to the table, whereas in other situations the trainees were able to go to client calls when they didn't source that opportunity themselves. That's something I did not understand. I was not given any feedback so basically I had to learn on my own while others were being taken under the wings of senior people and being shown how to create asset allocation models. I was given limited guidance where I could have easily made mistakes that could jeopardize my licenses or give an investment idea that was not suitable for the client.

"The members of my group, one colleague and the person

who ran the team, basically my supervisor, liked to play tennis. I like to play tennis occasionally. They would talk about instances where they would go play tennis, yet they never invited me. Even regular greetings in the morning where after you develop a relationship with someone you talk a bit more casually. You talk about the weekend, sports, etc. They were always very professional with me. They just usually said good morning to me. I attempted numerous times to develop relationships but I could see it was not welcomed.

"I really left because there was a better opportunity where I am now. Today, I work for a non-profit organization that trains and develops students of color who want to pursue careers in banking. At the same time the reason why I was seeking a new opportunity was because I just felt like the hurdle was not set for success; it was set for failure. Once I saw that the outcome of working there was not too bright, I started looking for other opportunities. My current position just fell in my lap.

"Had it not been for feeling like I was not getting trained or was not feeling welcomed in the team, I probably would have stayed in private banking and not looked for other opportunities. I stayed with the company for eight or nine months. It took me about two months to get my licenses, and then the other six months I was placed on a team. Then it became evident that it was not a good fit during the fourth month. I spoke with the woman who hired me and voiced my concern and she was very busy and basically told me to figure it out. But when I went back to the team, the dynamic was not there. Then it started getting really uncomfortable. There was never a conflict. It never got to that point."

❧ ❧

Tamika Lewiston* saw similar signs of sabotage to her career as a chemist. When she joined her company, she could not help but think, "It is 2004. Why am I the only black chemist in this company?" After a few years of traversing the bumpy and arduous terrain as the only black person, she understood why and left for higher ground. "I have felt like an outsider, not so much in my current job but in my previous job. I was the only black person who was a chemist for analytical sciences. It wasn't so much that I was a woman; I was just the only black person. There were a couple of instances where I was not copied on a couple of emails for test results and instrumentation. When the vice president specifically asked for test results, I just stood there with my mouth open because I was not copied on the original email from the boss, who was Puerto Rican. I tried to talk to the boss but she wasn't too responsive. So I figured that I would have a closed-door meeting with her. It turned into a confrontation instead of a conversation. She denied that she left me out of the loop and she denied that she did not copy me on the email. I felt like I wasn't even a part of the group. I felt like I didn't have a voice. I left that job in part because I felt like an outsider.

"The big difference in the previous job and my current job is that there are a lot more minorities in my department in general. When I was first hired, I was the only full-time woman, but I wasn't the only black person. We had a lot of diversity. We had a Jamaican man and a Vietnamese woman. Through the years we got a Russian man, we got another woman who was half Vietnamese and half Cambodian. We have a guy who is from the Dominican Republic. We have a guy from Scotland. We have a guy who is Filipino and a Chinese man. And that's just a handful of our diversity, and that makes a big difference.

"You don't feel as ostracized because of your race because there is a lot of diversity. The boss that I had when I first was hired, he never saw color or sex. I just happened to be the only woman by chance. He always focused on who was the most qualified."

⊷ ⊷

ADVICE FOR MANAGERS

Recruitment is probably the number one strategy an organization can use to increase the diversity of the staff and organizational leadership. Organizations have figured out creative recruitment strategies, such as attending (and sponsoring) career fairs that attract prospective employees of color, women, Latinos, and the LGBT community. Organizations have also engaged in very aggressive (and expensive) advertising campaigns and sponsor events to assist with their recruitment strategies. These are typical approaches but do they really maximize the organization's ability to market itself to diverse communities? How much impact does sponsoring an awards banquet or placing an advertisement in a magazine have on a candidate who walks through your organization and sees that he or she will be the "only one" in a particular department?

Instead, organizations could develop or sponsor programs that give employees and students tangible employment skills and create a real impact on the lives of future employees. For instance, for Black History Month, I worked with White & Case, an international law firm, in presenting a seminar about career fulfillment for Columbia Law School's Black Law Student Association. In an informal setting, but within a purpose-driven conversation, the students had an opportunity to hear about life at the law firm as it related to their career goals.

The conversation definitely went beyond the law firm's brochure. The attorneys provided insight as to how they navigated their careers and made different decisions that often stump people when they enter the workplace. The students walked away feeling empowered with new information and felt less mind-blind. White & Case's profile was significantly elevated in the black law students' minds because they saw that the firm cared about their professional development regardless of where they decided to work. It was not just another networking event. These are the types of programs that truly show an investment in and attract diverse candidates. Organizations should also sincerely look to their employees for referrals for filling job openings and to participate in interviews and selection committees.

⇥ ⇤

Harvey Benitez* not only participates in his firm's hiring and selection committee but his presence also sets the tone for changing the firm's dangerous misperceptions about candidates of color. "Being a Latino lawyer it's difficult to interact with other Latinos or get qualified Latino candidates to be taken seriously. I am the sole Latino at my firm. There's just a sense in the Pacific Northwest, which is where I practice, that there just isn't a real effort to bring any critical mass of people together. I think the primary way I feel like an outsider is not having any Latino peers and when I do bring in qualified outstanding people of color they don't really get a chance. It is inordinately difficult to get attorneys of color hired. The firm says that it is looking for qualified candidates and when I do find them qualified candidates it always seems like there's a reason to not hire them: it's too late in the season, the candidate's grades aren't good, or the firm has already looked at other folks. The firm may bring people in for a screening interview but that's it.

"We have diversity speakers come into town and there was a Latino speaker and I was sitting at a table with people who were on the managing committee for the firm. I had a curious episode with a partner who was on the executive committee for the firm. His experience was that some minority groups, like Latinos, don't like to work at law firms or work at jobs that I believe would lead to a good career path. I found that that was some of the attitude. I told him that in my experiences, all kinds of law students from diverse backgrounds try to seek high-paying jobs that look good on their resumes and that will open jobs for their futures. He did not have a response.

"This made me feel like on some level there may have been good intentions but, especially with recruiting, the good intentions don't reflect in making good recruiting or lateral decisions. Even though people say they are interested in diversity, when I've brought specific people to the firm's attention, these candidates have not gotten a fair shake. It's frustrating. It doesn't make me feel like I have a long-term future with the firm. I don't think that it's likely that I'm going to succeed. I think that the firm tries to bring in diverse folks but they aren't taking all of the necessary steps to really make a change or a significant difference. The firm should be making sure that when people are available who are of diverse backgrounds that the firm makes a special effort to go get them, as opposed to having some other reason or excuse why they are not a good fit. Mostly in the recruiting part, that feels frustrating."

⤙⊨◉ ⟜◈⤚

Organizations that feel as though there are not enough diverse candidates to choose from could also be a part of the process for changing the situation and increasing the pipeline of diverse candidates. There are so many opportunities for organizations to create a presence in underserved communities with a minimal time commitment. For organizations that claim that they do not have the time or the resources to coordinate pipeline efforts, I would encourage you to create a community service officer position in your organization. This person would be tasked with organizing all of your organization's outreach efforts. In the alternative, consider hiring consulting firms to coordinate and manage your community service and pipeline programs. Pardon the shameless plug, but the not-for-profit arm of my firm, QUEST Educational Initiatives, has created professional development curriculums for inner-city schools. The only role an organization has to play is providing volunteers and notifying them of the one-hour volunteer sessions. That's right, an organization can help thousands of students a year by just investing one hour of time per employee.

ADVICE FOR PROFESSIONALS AND STUDENTS

The employees who make some of the best career decisions are the ones who did their homework about the company. If you are planning to work for an organization that has no or few minorities, try to ask as many questions as possible. Ask your school career counselor if he or she knows anything about this company, or if they can connect you to graduates who worked for the organization. Don't be shy about reaching out to your school alumni base and the local professional trade associations, especially those that focus on underrepresented groups.

Technology has opened the doors to accessing honest feedback about an organization. Blogs are vital for receiving information about the company from the people who know it best: their employees. Blogs provide news and information about the organization's hiring practices, diversity practices, and overall culture. Google is another great resource for learning more about the type of work the company does. You can find the latest news headlines about the company to see what is making it newsworthy. Conduct internet research to see what kinds of clients the firm or company represented and the projects they engaged in, and determine whether you would feel comfortable in this environment.

Unfortunately, hindsight is 20/20 and too many professionals regret that they skipped these steps to research their employers. Many lament that if they had taken some steps to learn more about the office culture, they would have learned that the organization was traditionally led by people who were opposed to change and have not yet bought into diversity. They realize after a few years or months on the job that diversity is merely a marketing tactic.

You should try to eliminate as many surprises from the work environment as you can before you walk through the door. Use the interview as an opportunity to ask questions about the organization's culture from the perspective that is most important to you. If demographic composition is important to you, then ask. If lifestyle and work assignments are important to you, then ask. Remember, you can say and ask anything that you want; the trick is how you phrase and position your comments and questions. During the interview, you should get a sense of whether you would like to work with the people you meet. If you realize during the interview that you are meeting people who take themselves too seriously, whereas you appreciate levity, this might not be the right environment for you.

Although there is comfort in numbers, you shouldn't be afraid to be the "only one." You may be the only one because you are in a highly specialized area where there aren't too many people of any background. Period. Ultimately, your attitude and perspective about the environment will influence your experience as the only one.

⟶⟐ ⟐⟵

For instance, Edward Rodriquez* and Luz Costa* had completely different experiences being the only employees from working-class backgrounds working amongst privileged employees.

Edward found that he was not only one of a handful of

Filipinos in his investment banking firm but he was also one of the few who came from a different socioeconomic background. Because of his attitude, he could never feel comfortable in his firm. "I think a lot of what I encountered in the workplace were very subtle forms of racism, but my experience was more about diversity in thought, and diversity not being appreciated in terms of socioeconomic status. I grew up in a low-income urban neighborhood. The majority of my co-workers, even those who were of color, didn't necessarily have my background. I felt like such a minority. I was the one who came from a background where I felt like I struggled to get to a place like Morgan Stanley that has a lot of the trappings of success and a lot of the privileges that come with being around a lot of money—and that always made me feel uncomfortable. And it still does."

⇢⇒ ⇐⇐

Luz Costa, on the other hand, determined that as long as she worked in an environment that was respectful and offered equal opportunities, the financial trappings of her new environment would not ensnarl her career development. "The only difference between my colleagues and me was that I came from very humble means. I've had to work my way up. In my first firm, there were a lot of people with a lot of wealth. Going to a cocktail party or the firm's summer outing or something like that, I saw that wealth and felt a little in awe of it; like 'Wow, there's so much money in this room; look at this fantastic multi-million-dollar pad in Manhattan, it's amazing.' Once you see it for the first time, you move on.

"We're human beings; it doesn't matter what the differences are in terms of socioeconomic backgrounds. It was not uncomfortable for me because people around me made me comfortable. You get past the wealth differences very quickly because the people I worked and socialized with were great human beings. To this day, I am still in touch with those folks from my first firm who were very wealthy, so we bridged any differences or the differences were irrelevant.

"There's one guy in particular who comes from a very wealthy family and we email each other occasionally about going to a basketball game together with our kids. Those barriers did not get in the way of friendships or other relationships, professional or otherwise. That was my experience. I can't tell you that we became close friends, but relationships did happen notwithstanding those differences.

"I've only had two jobs professionally: one at a law firm and one at a consulting firm. At both of those places I have felt very comfortable, actually, as a woman. I never had an issue gender-wise. I also felt very comfortable race-wise. I never felt uncomfortable because I was perhaps the only Hispanic in the room. Everybody around me was so professional and so attuned to diversity that it was not an issue at all. People were extremely supportive in every way."

For Luz, being the only one was not an issue.

⟞ ⟞

Lerleen Boudreaux* is another junior-level professional who refuses to allow her gender or any other minority characteristic to get in the way of her career. When she made the move from a small farm in Illinois to New York City, she was thrust into an entirely different lifestyle. While her colleagues talk about growing up in apartments and their boarding school experiences, she thinks twice about whether she wants to talk about milking cows and taking care of farm animals.

In addition to her rural upbringing, being a woman at times has its challenges but it has never stood in her way. "Sometimes it's odd to be the only woman in a meeting with ten or twelve men. I can't think of a specific instance where I was offended, but I do encounter investment banker mentalities. You know, the jocular references. For instance, they use terms like 'open kimono' when you're discussing open disclosure of documents. I'm not offended by any of this because it's part of the environment. You can't be so thin skinned that you're always offended. There have been some instances where I have felt excluded but it was never anything horrible or blatant. I have never encountered anything that I have not been able to finesse."

⋯⫘ ⫘⋯

Being a trailblazer can be empowering and enjoyable, although it is hard work. As Elaine T. Jones, formerly of the NAACP Legal Defense Fund, says, "The job of the first is to keep the door open for others. If when you leave things haven't changed, then you have not done what you were supposed to do."

⋯⫘ ⫘⋯

Nydia Torres* was one of the only Latinos in her organization. She used her employer's limited views about Hispanics to her advantage and created inroads for all other Latinos in the organization. "I felt isolated many times, but it also challenged me to take on the role as a Latina spokesperson and utilize it to help my community and move up in the organization. Because there were so few of us in the organization, it made me more aware of the importance—even if we don't want to—of taking on that role to advance our community. And as a result of that, I did some pioneering work at that organization and three years later they've expanded my role into a national high-level position that serves the purpose of increasing the number of Latinos in the organization and servicing Latino people through the organization. So, it became a good thing. What was once an isolating incident became a good thing."

⟨⟨⟨⟨

Junior and mid-level professionals play a huge part in changing diversity in organizations by taking the time to figure out what concrete steps they can take to make a difference. Of course, you should do a good job and create a track record demonstrating that talent and skill come from employees of all different backgrounds. Minority employees can assist with recruitment by staying on the lookout for other minority candidates. Although you might not be able to attend every recruitment event, try to contact your alma mater and the leaders of the campus affinity groups and let them know that your company is making a recruiting visit. These resources can help you spread the word to students from underrepresented backgrounds and encourage them to stop by your company's booth, submit a resume, or interview for a position.

Minority professionals can also encourage their companies and firms to support minority professional trade organizations and their events. Although you may not have a great deal of influence within your workplace, you can assist with programming or at least make the necessary introductions between the leaders of your company and the professional trade organization.

What ideas do you have for improving diversity within your firm? In the space provided, try to jot down a few of your ideas for ensuring that there are fewer and fewer "only ones" in your organization. Try to be as specific as possible by determining time lines, the names of people who can assist you, and what initiatives you would like to see your firm implement. By taking these moves you will be keeping the door open for others and doing what you're supposed to do.

NOTES AND IDEAS

ENDING ON A HIGH NOTE

In 1993's *The Rage of a Privileged Class*, Ellis Cose wrote that "no other racial group in America had endured as much rejection on the path to acceptance" as African-Americans, and were left staring at the "final door" "uncertain of admittance." He examined the issues African-Americans in the middle class faced and drew attention to the disenfranchisement they continue to experience and the resulting rage they feel when they are left standing outside the "final door."

Looking at the situation fourteen years later by interviewing a broader swath of women and racial, cultural, religious, and other minorities, I see convincing arguments that while much has changed, much has remained the same.

In 2003, the Supreme Court of the United States recognized the importance of diversity in today's businesses in the University of Michigan admission case *Grutter v. Bollinger.* In its decision the Court stated, "American businesses have made clear that the skills needed in today's increasingly global marketplace can only be developed through exposure to widely diverse people, cultures, ideas, and viewpoints."

If television were society's diversity barometer, there would be very little room to argue that America is not a melting pot. Television shows like "My Wife and Kids" and "Grey's Anatomy" feature African-American, Asian, and Latino characters as positive role models. Angela Bassett, Danny Glover, and Gabrielle Union are just some of Hollywood's finest television personalities and actors.

Kenneth Chenault of American Express, Tracey Edmonds of Our Stories Films, and Richard Parsons of Time Warner are just a few of the African-American Chief Executive Officers in the financial services and entertainment industries.

The lesbian, gay, bisexual, and transgender (LGBT) community is starting to gain more acceptance by mainstream society. In a January 1997 *Newsweek* survey, more than 84% of Americans opposed employment discrimination on the basis of sexual orientation. In early 2000, gay men were a mainstream phenomenon with network television shows like "Will and Grace" and "Queer Eye for the Straight Guy." In 2005, after much delay, MTV launched Logo, a 24-hour television network featuring entertainment programming for the lesbian, gay, bisexual, and transgendered community. Now, there is a movement where straight men are more in touch with their stylish sides such that the term "metrosexual" was coined. In a surprising turn, the Supreme Court struck down a Texas law that made gay sex a crime in *Lawrence and Garner v. Texas*. In 2002, New York State passed the Sexual Orientation Non-Discrimination Act (SONDA), which prohibits discrimination against gays and lesbians in employment and housing. The Episcopal Church has even appointed its first openly gay bishop, the Reverend Gene Robinson.

The face of New York City's police department is also starting to reflect the religious diversity of our communities. In
2004, Sikhs won the right to wear their turbans while direct-
ing traffic as Traffic Enforcement Agents.

Women have also made considerable gains in society.
According to a Breakingtheglassceiling.com study, 85% of Fortune 500 companies have at least one woman on its board of
directors. The Census Bureau reported that over half a million
small businesses were owned and operated by African-American women. Over half of today's law students are women.

For over 40 years the Civil Rights Act of 1964 has made it
unlawful for an employer to discriminate on the basis of race,
color, religion, gender, and national origin. And, for over 10
years, the Americans with Disabilities Act has made it unlawful
to flat-out deny an employee with a disability employment.

In recent years, companies have stressed the importance
of recruiting more women and racial minorities, whether the
motivation is marketplace competition or voluntary moral
obligation. This is all impressive.

However, has the business case for diversity yielded a significant change in the workplace? Have we truly reached the
point where all Americans are treated equally, and discussions
about diversity and equal access to opportunities are unnecessary? Are there still people standing outside of the "final
door"?

Each year, thousands of employees file employment discrimination claims with the Equal Employment Opportunity
Commission. Since 2000, there has been an increase in retaliation cases.

While women have made considerable gains, we have not
yet reached economic parity with men. According to a boston.
com article titled "Top Wall Street Jobs Still Elude Women,
Minorities," women and racial minorities still have not pierced

those managing director level and above senior positions that reap multimillion-dollar bonuses. According to the U.S. Government Accountability Office, African-Americans only represent 6.6% of management, and white women comprise a little more than one third.

It's no secret that successful women often sacrifice having a family for their careers. A 2006 *New York Times* article, "Scant Progress on Closing Gap in Women's Pay," reported that in 2005 college-educated women between 36 and 45 years old earned 74.7 cents in hourly pay for every dollar that men in the same group did. One of the theories in the article to explain the pay disparity was, "[i]f the government offered day-care programs similar to those in other countries or men spent more time caring for family members, women would have greater opportunity to pursue whatever job they wanted."

In 2005, Neil French, a senior advertising executive with the WPP Group, the biggest advertising agency in the world, declared at a conference, "women don't make it to the top because they don't deserve to. They're crap!" He explained that our roles as caregivers and child bearers prevent us from succeeding in top positions. Female CEOs of the largest advertising agencies earn an average of $40,000 less than their male counterparts.

Women are not the only underrepresented group in the advertising world. The New York City Commission on Human Rights took a look at the demographics of 16 advertising agencies and was startled. Blacks made up only 2.5% of the upper echelon in New York's advertising firms.

In law firms, blacks and Hispanics comprise less than 20% of the attorneys in prestigious law firms. According to a Catalyst study, minority partners account for only 3% of partners in the nation's law firms.

Even in everyday living, African-Americans are subjected to disparate treatment. In 2006, America watched Michael Richards, who played the wacky character Kramer on television's "Seinfeld," spiral out of control on a racist rant against African-Americans in a nightclub.

A 2003 study found that African-American and Hispanic women have a greater likelihood of dying from diabetes, poverty, and as victims of violence than Caucasian women.

In New York and Washington D.C., studies have cited that blacks still experience difficulty hailing a cab. In 2000, there were 3,529 complaints about unlawful refusals in New York. In Washington D.C., 94 citations were issued against taxi drivers who passed by black undercover officers in favor of white officers posing as customers.

In housing, undercover testing revealed that a City University of New York law student was refused an apartment because of his race. The landlord stated, "My neighbors would slit my throat if I rented to a black man."

And even the media's description of a news story is sometimes biased by what you look like, instead of what you did to make the news. Remember the coverage of 2005's hurricane Katrina? Black "survivors" *looted* from grocery stores, while white "residents" *found* food from local grocery stores.

Despite the increase of gay-focused newspapers and magazines in the United States, the gay community is still marginalized by mainstream heterosexual society. In a survey posted on breakingtheglassceiling.com, 191 employers revealed that 18% would fire, 27% would refuse to hire, and 26% would refuse to promote a person they perceived to be lesbian, gay, or bisexual. Jerry Thacker, a Christian activist chosen by the Bush administration for an AIDS advisory panel, characterized the disease as the "gay plague." In New York State and most other states, the discrimination statutes do not include the transgender community.

The creators of Facebook, which describes itself as "a social utility that connects people with friends and others who work, study and live around them," probably never imagined that overprotective parents of college students would use their innovation as a dam in the stream of diversity. Parents across the United States are starting to use Facebook to change their children's roommate assignments. According to a 2007 *USA Today* article, "a growing number of schools say they're getting more requests for changes—from parents who don't like the roommates' Facebook profiles." One college official cited race, religion, and sexual orientation as the top reasons for parents having concerns about the housing assignments. One school received a call from a parent who had "psychological and sanitary concerns" about a student's new roommates, both of whom were gay men.

Although America's first European settlers were in search of religious freedoms, religious tolerance is often a concept and not a practice. During the 2003 New York City Marathon, a 92-year-old Sikh running along the 26-mile route was taunted for wearing a turban and told he resembled Osama Bin Laden. During Yom Kippur, Jewish neighborhoods in New York were vandalized with swastikas and slashed tires. From September 11, 2001, to February 14, 2003, the FBI opened 414 hate crime investigations involving attacks or threats against Arab-American targets, resulting in more than 140 prosecutions. In total, there were 7,462 crime incidents reported to the FBI in 2002, and 9,730 reported in 2001.

Based on the newspaper articles, media coverage, research health studies, and comedic outbursts, we are far from the point where it is no longer necessary to have affinity groups or focus on the recruitment, retention, and advancement of people of color, women and other underrepresented minorities in the workplace. Despite anti-discrimination laws and public displays of diversity, harassment and discrimination still exist in the workplace.

The successful people from African-American, Asian, Latino, and other backgrounds that I spoke with did all the right things academically and professionally but were still undermined, overlooked, and underestimated in the workplace. Instead of partying many nights in high school and college they studied hard to make the honor roll or the Dean's List. They spent their summers working in competitive internships for little or no pay. All of the people I interviewed were hard-working, talented, and beautiful people who were excluded from the inner-workings of their organizations. After graduating from the right schools; working nights, weekends, and holidays; and making other sacrifices in their personal lives, they were disappointed when they realized they were not fully accepted by their supervisors and colleagues.

If the people I interviewed were enraged, it was obscured by the satisfaction they enjoy by being their own business owners. Many of the people I interviewed are a part of the growing number of people of color who are gladly becoming masters of their own destiny.

According to the National Supplier Diversity Council, a non-profit group that matches minority-owned businesses with major corporations in search of goods and services, African-Americans, Asian Americans, Hispanic Americans, and Native Americans are all starting their own businesses at a much faster rate than the average for overall U.S. businesses. In 2006, some of America's biggest companies purchased more than $100 billion worth of goods and services from minority-owned companies. This is a dramatic leap from when the NMSDC got its start 35 years ago. Back then, American companies spent less than $100 million with minority-owned firms.

Many presidents and CEOs of minority-owned companies started their careers in corporate America, but found their way to small business ownership. Sam Hamadeh, founder and chief executive of Vault.com, provided a poignant explanation for the dramatic increase in minority entrepreneurship in the December 2006 issue of Knowledge @Wharton. He brought attention to the fact that "[B]eing an outsider increases the likelihood that someone will want to start his own venture. The more you are a part of the establishment, the more you are giving up to start a business."

Many of the individuals who participated in this book are highly accomplished women and men who left their organizations to be successful elsewhere. When I interviewed them, I felt their disappointment and acknowledgement that they were duped into believing that they would ever be invited to cross the threshold of the final door. However, instead of feeling anger or rage when they could not cross the threshold of someone else's final door, they created their own final door. The people I spoke with used their rage to fuel small businesses and other alternative ventures. Instead of stewing in anger when they were denied access, they got mad and then took action. They decided to work for the competition or start their own companies.

I could relate completely with many of the Generation Xers and Yers that I interviewed. I thought that all of my hard work would have amounted to a successful career in the law and eventually a partnership track. However, I went through seven years as an attorney feeling isolated, not mentored, outside of the network, and perceived as underqualified. With the right training, mentoring, and work assignments, who knows what kind of attorney I might have become? If I worked in an environment free of cultural insensitivity, stereotypes, and aggressive communication, I might have actually enjoyed working for someone else. And, had I been coached through my mistakes and given the opportunity to learn immediately as opposed to subsequently, I might have churned out masterpiece briefs.

Alas, everything happens for a good reason. It is no mistake that any of these things happened *for* me. After practicing employment law for six years I had an "aha" moment about what I wanted to be when I grew up. While facilitating a leadership training session for an organization that trains and develops students of color into business tycoons, I realized how much I enjoyed creating educational programs about employment rights and responsibilities in the workplace. I preferred to proactively work with groups to create employment education programs that focus on the intersection of diversity issues and career management instead of engaging in hardcore adversarial courtroom battles. So as to not delay the dream, I created my own diversity consulting firm—QUEST Diversity Initiatives—and made the permanent switch from practicing law. Today, the majority of my work as a diversity consultant involves working with corporations, law firms, educational institutions, and community-based organizations to approach diversity by Questioning their Understood Established Societal Training.

My experiences caused me to grow and become entrepreneurial by starting my own diversity consulting firm. I have not looked back at what could have been.

INDEX

ABOUT NATALIE HOLDER-WINFIELD
Diversity & Employment Law Consultant

NATALIE HOLDER-WINFIELD is an experienced employment lawyer who proactively works with corporations, law firms, educational institutions, and non-profit organizations to meet their workforce training needs. As QUEST's Diversity & Employment Consultant, she uses recent legal precedents to create realistic customized training videos and training programs. Since 2003, she has created seminars for over 2,000 students and professionals in such organizations as Time Warner, the New York City Bar, the Louisiana State Bar Association, INROADS, Connecticut Regional Water Authority and KeySpan Energy. In addition to organizational training, she practiced discrimination law in government and law firm settings. As a litigator, Ms. Holder-Winfield prosecuted cases of employment, housing, and public accommodation discrimination. She successfully litigated a landmark religious accommodation case against the New York City Police Department, changing the uniform policy for Sikhs. In 2004, the International Bar Association (IBA) invited her to its annual conference in Auckland, New Zealand, to present her article "Diversity in the Workplace from a Law Enforcement Perspective," published in the November 2004 IBA Journal. In 2007, she was appointed Vice Chair of the Minorities in the Profession Committee of the Young Lawyers Division of the American Bar Association (ABA), and was named a Labor and Employment Fellow for the ABA's Alternative Dispute Resolution Committee.

Ms. Holder-Winfield is member of NYU's Young Alumni Leadership Circle and a variety of bar associations. Ms. Holder-Winfield is admitted to practice in New York and Connecticut. She is a graduate of Tulane Law School and New York University.

Contact: natalie@qeinitiatives.org

READER RESPONSE

We would appreciate your comments regarding *Recruiting and Retaining a Diverse Workforce: New Rules for a New Generation*. If you have any comments or suggestions, please let us know. Please mail or fax this response form to:

Reader Response Department
First Books
6750 SW Franklin, Suite A
Portland, OR 97223-2542
Fax: 503.968.6779

Comments: _____

_____

_____

_____

_____

_____

_____

_____

Name: _____

Title: _____

Address: _____

_____

Telephone: (   ) _____

Email: _____

6750 SW Franklin, Suite A
Portland, OR 97223-2542
USA
P: 503.968.6777
www.firstbooks.com

FIRST BOOKS

MOVING WITH KIDS?

Look into *The Moving Book: A Kids' Survival Guide*.

Divided into three sections (before, during, and after the move), it's a handbook, a journal, and a scrapbook all in one. Includes address book, colorful change-of-address cards, and a useful section for parents.

Children's Book of the Month Club "Featured Selection"; American Bookseller's "Pick of the List"; Winner of the Family Channel's "Seal of Quality" Award

And for your younger children, ease their transition with our brand-new title just for them, *Max's Moving Adventure: A Coloring Book for Kids on the Move*. A complete story book featuring activities as well as pictures that children can color; designed to help children cope with the stresses of small or large moves.

GOT PETS?

The Pet Moving Handbook: Maximize Your Pet's Well-Being and Maintain Your Sanity by Carrie Straub answers all your pet-moving questions and directs you to additional resources that can help smooth the move for both you and your pets.

"Floats to the top, cream of the crop. Awesome book; I'm going to keep one on the special shelf here." – Hal Abrams, Animal Radio

NEWCOMER'S HANDBOOKS®

Regularly revised and updated, these popular guides are now available for Atlanta, Boston, Chicago, London, Los Angeles, Minneapolis–St. Paul, New York City, Portland, San Francisco Bay Area, Seattle, Texas and Washington DC.

"Invaluable ...highly recommended" – *Library Journal*

If you're coming from another country, don't miss the *Newcomer's Handbook® for Moving to and Living in the USA* by Mike Livingston, termed "a fascinating book for newcomers and residents alike" by the *Chicago Tribune*.

BUSINESS WRITING RESOURCES

The Art of On-the-Job Writing by Philip Vassallo offers a unique, integrated method for achieving workplace-writing success. This easy-to-use guidebook provides real-life case studies and numerous practice opportunities. Phil's *The Art of E-Mail Writing* will help your employees write clear, concise, purposeful, and thorough e-mails faster, while better managing the entire e-process.

FIRST BOOKS

6750 SW Franklin Street
Portland, Oregon 97223-2542
Phone 503.968.6777 • Fax 503.968.6779
www.firstbooks.com

Printed in the United States
112840LV00002B/9/A